Moses

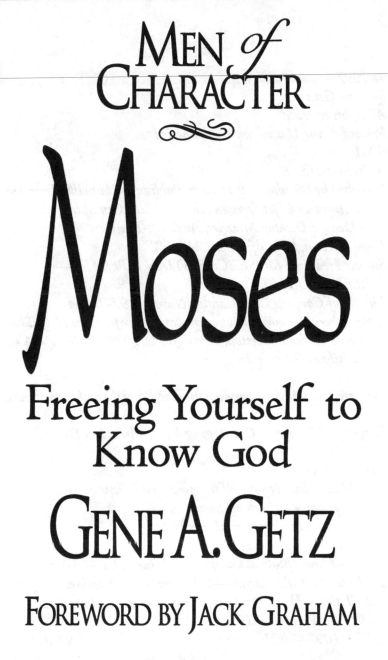

MEN *of* CHARACTER

Moses

Freeing Yourself to Know God

GENE A. GETZ

FOREWORD BY JACK GRAHAM

BROADMAN
&HOLMAN
PUBLISHERS
Nashville, Tennessee

© 1997
by Gene Getz
All rights reserved
Printed in the United States of America
4261–69
0–8054–6169–8
Published by Broadman & Holman Publishers, Nashville, Tennessee
Acquisitions and Development Editor: Vicki Crumpton
Page Design: Desktop Miracles, Addison, Texas
Dewey Decimal Classification: 248.842
Subject Heading: MOSES/CHRISTIAN LIFE/MEN—
    RELIGIOUS LIFE
Library of Congress Card Catalog Number: 97-22584
Unless otherwise noted, Scripture quotations are from the Holy Bible,
New International Version, copyright © 1973, 1978, 1984 by
International Bible Society.

Italicized words in Scripture quotations indicate the author's emphasis.

Library of Congress Cataloging-in-Publication Data

Getz, Gene A.
    Moses : freeing yourself to know God / Gene A. Getz
        p. cm. — (Men of character)
    Includes bibliographical references.
    ISBN 0–8054–6169–8
    1. Moses (Biblical leader)   2. Bible. O.T.—Biography.
3. Bible. O.T. Pentateuch—Criticism, interpretation, etc.
    I. Title.   II. Series: Getz, Gene A. Men of character.
    BS580.M6G446   1997
    222'.1092—dc21   97-22584
                                                        CIP

    2 3 4 5   01 00

*I*n many respects, this book on Moses' life focuses on how to be a great leader. This is why I want to dedicate this publication to my good friend and fellow pastor, Jack Graham. He was called to shepherd and lead Prestonwood Baptist Church in Dallas, Texas, at a critical moment in the life of this great church and has demonstrated unusual faith, wisdom, and leadership skills in guiding this congregation to become one of the most dynamic churches in America. Thanks, Jack, for your leadership model. It's a privilege to dedicate this book to you and also to serve with you as a fellow pastor in one of the great and needy mission fields in the United States—the Dallas Metroplex!

Contents

Foreword

I first met Gene Getz at a men's Bible study/ski retreat in Beaver Creek, Colorado. After years of knowing and respecting him via the printed page, it was my privilege to get to know him up close. Not only was I inspired by his well-known ability to teach the Word of God, but I was immediately taken with the warmth of his personality and the depth of his spiritual walk. Here was a man's man who was also God's man. How refreshing when your spiritual heroes are everything and more than you had hoped them to be.

We all need heroes. In a society where celebrities are honored, and even at times worshiped, we are often deeply disappointed with their behavior and irresponsible lifestyles. So we long for leaders whose character matches their reputation.

Moses is such a leader. The man who led millions of Israelites out of bondage in Egypt and subsequently delivered the Ten Commandments has shaped society like no other man in history other than the God-Man, Jesus. The human author of the first five books of the Bible, Moses laid the foundations of our faith and introduced the world to the eternal God of the ages.

Gene Getz allows us to look inside the life and character of this renowned prophet, and with keen insight, he enables us to learn from the life of this incredible man.

Moses is often perceived as a man of the Law. Some see him as a stern, austere religious relic from the past. But Gene Getz gives us an opportunity to know the real Moses; a man who knew disappointment as well as elation; a leader who experienced God on the mountain top, but also walked with Him through the wilderness. It is good—very good—to realize our God can use us in spite of our own failures if we are willing to know Him truly and do His will. Moses, the Law-giver, points us to the Life-giver, Jesus. He leads us to Christ and explains our desperate need of grace, mercy, and forgiveness. Indeed, his testimony of faith speaks to us to this very day.

Every sincere, Spirit-led Christian wants to know, How can God use me? How can I become a faithful servant of God and use my influence for Christ? Can God use me to touch lives and lead people to love and obey the Word of God? This book will enable the reader to discover the joyous fact that God calls and uses ordinary people in extraordinary ways when we are committed to Him. Moses heard and surrendered to the call of the great I Am at a burning bush in the desert. My prayer is that this book will be a "burning bush" in which all who read will encounter the God of Moses and yield to His unmistakable call.

Bless you, Gene Getz, and thank you for your faithful ministry of explaining the Scriptures and enabling the great men of the Bible to step from the pages of Scripture and into our hearts. You have helped us to know God and to become men and women of character.

Dr. Jack Graham
Pastor, Prestonwood Baptist Church
Dallas, Texas

Moses: A Man Who Will Touch Your Life

I've studied and written about a number of Old Testament personalities, but no other has impacted my life like Moses. This should not surprise you or me. When the final words were added to the story of his life, it was said: "Since then, no prophet has risen in Israel like Moses, whom the LORD knew face to face" (Deut. 34:10).

Think for a moment what this really means. Moses was a man who literally walked and talked with God. In turn, the Lord spoke to him "face to face, as a man speaks with his friend" (Exod. 33:11). No leader in Israel ever experienced God's presence like Moses. After speaking with the Lord on Mount Sinai, his own face was radiant with God's glory and goodness (34:29).

But remember, Moses was just a man. He was not the God-Man. Only Jesus Christ is both perfect God and perfect man. Moses had all of the human weaknesses that characterize any son of Adam. Though he was beautiful from birth, was highly educated in all the wisdom of Egypt, and developed into a great orator and leader, Moses made a serious mistake that left him intimidated and fearful. He lost his self-confidence and had difficulty expressing himself. His self-image dropped below zero, and he suffered from a serious inferiority complex.

It was at this moment in his life that God spoke to him from a burning bush, empowered him, began the process of rebuilding his self-image, and then sent him back to face the Pharaoh of Egypt and to perform "all those miraculous signs and wonders" (Deut. 34:11). Moses led the children of Israel out of Egypt, across the Red Sea, and to the foot of Mt. Sinai, where God revealed Himself as never before. Moses entered into the very presence of God and received the Ten Commandments and delivered them on tablets of stone to all Israel.

It's not only Moses' relationship with God that gripped my own soul. It was his incredible loyalty to God's people. He was a shepherd without equal, interceding for all Israel when God became so angry with their idolatry and immorality that He wanted to wipe them off the face of the earth. He actually offered to give his own life for his "wayward sheep." On several occasions, Moses' prayerful intercession was so great that the sovereign God of the universe actually "relented" or "changed His mind"—something I can only accept by faith. But there's one thing I do understand: God honors faith and sincere prayer and listens when we cry out to Him for help and assistance!

There are many things throughout Moses' life and ministry that have impacted my own, but these two stand out: I want to get to know God better, and I want to be a more faithful servant to God's people. As you read and study Moses' life, I'm confident God will speak to you too. There are great lessons for us all!

Chapter 1

A Family Crisis
Read Exodus 1:1–2:10

*N*ever in the history of our society have we witnessed more family crises. Unfortunately, some happen simply because of human error. The very week I wrote the introduction to this chapter, a small boy was suddenly killed when an air bag exploded in his face as his mother swerved the car she was driving and hit a curb. Sadly, the young lad wasn't wearing a seat belt, leaving his head and shoulders totally exposed to the impact. That evening as I watched a brokenhearted father share on the news what had happened, my own heart grieved for this family—especially for the mother, who will probably be tempted to blame herself the rest of her life for this accident.

Other family tragedies—perhaps most of them—are more directly related to evil and sin in the world. Oftentimes children suffer because of the decisions of wicked, selfish people who are more concerned about their own status in life than the welfare of others. Consider the horrible results of war. Nothing is more tragic than to see innocent children terribly maimed or killed. Just this week I saw a young lad who had lost his eyesight in a war-torn country. Feeling a deep sense of anxiety and loss, he whispered to his father that he would have been better off if he had been killed.

These stories, and many like them, are gripping. They demonstrate that life is fragile. But there are other stories that can be told in which God in His sovereign grace has provided miraculous care and protection—particularly in response to faith and courage. The story of Moses illustrates this wonderful reality.

An Outright Assault

The account of Moses' birth and survival is an amazing story of faith, courage, and clear thinking during a time of great political upheaval in Egypt. Amram and Jochebed, Moses' parents, faced an incredible crisis. The Pharaoh of Egypt, responding to his own sense of threat and fear, ordered that all newborn males in Israel be snatched from their mothers' breasts and thrown into the Nile River (Exod. 1:22). Jochebed gave birth to Moses during this turbulent moment in Israel's history. From a human point of view, it would be just a matter of time before Moses was discovered, facing certain death! But as we'll see, God intervened and responded to courageous faith.

Four Centuries Earlier

Moses' story is a sequel to Joseph's life. Joseph was one of the twelve sons of Jacob, and because he was a favorite son, his brothers hated him. But rather than kill him as they originally had intended, they sold him to a band of Midianite merchants who transported him to Egypt where he was put on a slave block. Through a series of God-ordained events, Joseph was freed from slavery and rose to a position of prime minister in Egypt. In this significant role, he prepared the people of Egypt for a great famine—so widespread that it also affected his family back in Canaan. Because Joseph was respected by Pharaoh, he was able to bring his whole family, consisting of seventy people, down to Egypt. Here they settled on a beautiful and fertile section of land where they could live in peace and plenty (Gen. 45:16–20).

But life was not always to be tranquil for the children of Israel. Time has a way of blurring memories, changing circumstances, and hardening the hearts of men.

From Seventy to Two Million

For more than four hundred years, "the Israelites were fruitful and multiplied greatly and became exceedingly numerous, so that the land was filled with them" (Exod. 1:7). From a small beginning numbering seventy people, this little band of people became a great nation—probably numbering in excess of two million. However, as is so often true in life, what sometimes begins as a great blessing can become a great burden— even a curse.

Four hundred years is a long time. Joseph's great exploits in Egypt were forgotten, "lost" in the continuing events of history. Pharaoh's promises to Israel were also forgotten. The scriptural record is clear: "A new king, who did not know about Joseph, came to power in Egypt" (1:8).

The phrase "a new king" evidently refers to a monarch who differed substantially in his philosophy of leadership and who departed from his predecessors' policies and principles. In fact, the Scriptures imply he was not even interested in the "way" the previous kings ruled Egypt. Consequently, when we read that this king "did not know about Joseph," it is also implied that he really didn't care to know anything about the man whose name had become a household word in the archives of Egypt. This Pharaoh was interested in building a reputation for himself, not perpetuating the exploits of a predecessor— especially the achievements of a Hebrew named Joseph.

The new king's attitude toward Israel's growth rate allows us to peer into his personality. He was an insecure and threatened man. In typical paranoid fashion, he exaggerated and projected his fears. "'Look,' he said to his people, 'the Israelites have become much too numerous for us'" (1:9).

Actually, Pharaoh had two concerns. First, if there was a war, he was afraid Israel might join forces with Egypt's enemies. Second, if this should happen, the children of Israel might leave Egypt (1:10). For Pharaoh, this was a catch-22. He wasn't comfortable living with the Israelites, but neither was he comfortable living without them.

The Acts of a Threatened Man

Even though Pharaoh was at the helm, he was not thinking clearly. His attempts to curtail Israel's growth rate came in three stages that were more emotional than rational.

Ruthless Demoralization

The Pharaoh first tried to demoralize the Israelites. His goal was to wear them down in both body and soul so that they would stop reproducing at such a rapid rate. He "put slave masters over them to oppress them with forced labor" (1:11).

Theoretically, this kind of hard work should reduce the birthrate. But ironically, the harder these men worked, the more children they produced—which only served to raise the threat level throughout Egypt. Consequently, more pressure was put on the Israelites. The biblical record speaks for itself: "But the more they were oppressed, the more they multiplied and spread; so the Egyptians came to dread the Israelites and worked them ruthlessly. They made their lives bitter with hard labor in brick and mortar and with all kinds of work in the fields; in all their hard labor the Egyptians used them ruthlessly" (1:12–14).

Murderous Birth Control

Since the Pharaoh's initial plan didn't work, he went to plan B. It was a wicked and terrible strategy, one that could only be contrived in the heart of a ruthless, egotistical man who was terribly weak on the inside and all façade on the outside. In order to curtail the birthrate, the Pharaoh decided to kill outright all the newborn sons of Israel. In his evil mind, the king reasoned that if hard work wouldn't stop procreation, the ruthless destruction of newborn males would. Who would feel free to bring a child into the world when there was a 50/50 probability that the child would be killed?

But the Pharaoh's diabolical plot failed the second time. The midwives who were ordered to kill all the male children at birth were more loyal to God than to the king of Egypt (1:15–17). Though they told only a half-truth when confronted by the king, God still honored the deeper motives of their hearts. They risked their own lives to save the newborn baby boys in Israel. Consequently, God honored and blessed them (1:18–21).

Heartless Infanticide

In a final frenzied third step, the king ordered every young male to be thrown "into the Nile" (1:22). Imagine the weeping and wailing among the families of Israel as newborn infants were snatched from their mothers' breasts and thrown into the murky waters of this Egyptian river.

In the midst of this severe crisis, Moses was born. It's at this moment we're able to watch a family face this terrifying situation head on—with faith, courage, and a unique strategy that made Pharaoh's behavior stand out for what it was: emotional, egocentric, fearful, immoral, and irrational.

Facing the Crisis

Moses' parents, Amram and Jochebed, were both from the tribe of Levi (Exod. 2:1; 6:20). They grew up in a pagan and wicked environment—not only among the Egyptians but among their kinfolk. After living in Egypt for more than four hundred years and watching the Egyptians worship their heathen deities and engage in evil practices, most of the children of Israel became like their pagan counterparts.

This evil influence lingered on for years to come. This is why Joshua, even after they had settled in the land of Canaan, charged Israel to "fear the Lord" and to "throw away the gods" their "forefathers worshiped . . . *in Egypt*" (Josh. 24:14). The sinful practices these people had learned in this pagan culture were so entrenched in their hearts and minds that they appeared years later in their children. Remember, too, that this kind of idolatry and immorality took place even *after* God had appeared to Israel at Mt. Sinai and had revealed His divine Laws.

For some unstated reason, Moses' parents had remained true to the God of Israel. They had not forsaken the Lord to worship false gods. Consequently, when Moses was born in the midst of this tremendous crisis, Amram and Jochebed trusted God to preserve this little boy's life.

Faith That Works

The author of Hebrews lets us in on a very important aspect of Moses' parents' approach to solving this problem—an aspect assumed but omitted in the Old Testament record. They turned to God, trusting Him to help them save Moses from what appeared to be certain death. We read: "*By faith* Moses' parents hid him for three months after he was born, because they saw he was no ordinary child" (Heb. 11:23).

After citing their faith in the midst of the crisis, the author of Hebrews went on to say that "they were not *afraid* of the king's edict" (11:23b). Their faith also generated courage!

Imagine the first three months. For nearly one hundred days, they hid their beautiful child and guarded his crib. Jochebed probably nursed him more than necessary just to make sure that Moses did not cry out because of hunger—crying out could have brought sudden death.

Moses' parents certainly had a lot of fear. At any moment the Egyptian soldiers could have snatched Moses away from Jochebed and cast him into the Nile River. Any normal parent would have been petrified every moment of every day. But this was not the case. Though both Amram and Jochebed must have experienced normal anxiety, their faith in God dissipated the immobilizing fear that at times takes over in the midst of this kind of horrible crisis.

Imagine what would have happened if this little family had panicked. They would have lost their ability to think and act rationally. However, it was their faith, courage, and calm approach that enabled them to develop a strategic plan to preserve Moses' life.

An Amazing Plan

The time came when Amram and Jochebed could no longer hide Moses. Being a normal child, Moses began to take on the characteristics of an active and growing boy. The danger that he might be discovered became too great. His parents knew that they had to take action and implement a plan they had probably thought about for weeks, going over and over again the possible outcomes.

Jochebed tarred a small basket and made it waterproof. She then placed her baby in the basket and took him directly to the very means of death itself—the Nile River (Exod. 2:3). How ironic! They believed that the place where children were being murdered could become a source of life. They theorized that the Egyptian soldiers would never look for live babies in the Nile river. They were right!

But there was another dimension to this ingenious plan. Jochebed chose a particular place in the Nile River because she knew that Pharaoh's daughter came there to bathe regularly. Obviously, they had studied her patterns—what day, what time of day, how long, and so forth. Why not put Moses where he could be found by a person who could save his life—the daughter of the very man who had issued the death edict in the first place? Hoping against hope, they trusted God to cause the princess to find Moses gently floating "among the reeds." Furthermore, they trusted God to cause Pharaoh's daughter to be attracted to little Moses.

The Plan Unfolds

When Pharaoh's daughter arrived on the scene and saw the little basket bobbing up and down in the river, she was instantly curious and had one of her servants retrieve it. To her amazement, she gazed on a beautiful little boy and immediately recognized him as one of the Hebrew children. She knew why he was there. How could she not be aware of her father's evil nature and insidious plot? Consequently, when she opened the basket and saw little Moses crying, she felt compassion (2:6)—a miracle indeed!

At this moment, we see another step in this ingenious plan unfold. As Pharaoh's daughter looked down at this hungry little baby, she naturally wondered what to do next. Right on schedule, Moses' sister, Miriam, "suddenly appeared" and offered the princess a very practical solution. "Shall I go and get one of the Hebrew women to nurse the baby for you?" she asked (2:7).

To Pharaoh's daughter, this appeared as a coincidence. You and I know better. This was a strategy—carefully and cautiously thought out and prayed through for three months—and it was working beautifully.

What happened next is ironic—and almost humorous. Miriam brought Moses' mother, who took her little boy back into her arms to nurse him and to rear him—not for a few days, but for several years. Furthermore, Jochebed did it all with the protection of the daughter of the king of Egypt, the same king who had ordered Moses' death! Even more ironic, she was paid to mother her own child (2:9)!

Becoming God's Man Today

Principles to Live By

What do parents in our "enlightened" twentieth-century Western culture have in common with the Eastern culture that existed millennia ago? Are there any points of identification with Amram and Jochebed? One constant permeates all societies of the world and defies the element of time. Paul put it succinctly: "For all have sinned and fall short of the glory of God" (Rom. 3:23). The sin principle has been operative ever since Adam and Eve sinned in the Garden of Eden and has certainly affected family life ever since. The jealousy and hatred that caused Cain to kill Abel and that led to the paganism that permeated Egypt is still at work today in our sophisticated culture. We battle the same influences within the world's system.

Principle 1. Parents living in today's world must be alert to the dangers in our own society that are attempting to destroy our children.

As Christian parents, we're living in the midst of an environment that can be very detrimental to our children. Dangers lurk everywhere! Some of these dangers are far from subtle.

Sex Offenders

It's no secret that pedophiles roam the streets—some dressed in business suits and carrying briefcases! Furthermore, these men are being released from prison in record numbers.

Today I read an article in the paper regarding a man who is being released from prison early who has openly stated he has no control over his urges to abuse little children sexually. While in prison, he actually asked to be castrated. But the state denied his request. And now that he is being released early because of good behavior, he is still requesting this operation. Ironically, he is trying to protect children from what he knows is a terrible temptation to harm them.

However, those in charge of making such decisions are wavering and struggling with the issue—wondering what to do!

Think, however, of the thousands of people who are at large with no desire whatsoever to curtail their activities. They lie awake nights, thinking of how they can seduce little children. Never before in the history of our society have we faced such a terrible plague! Unfortunately, we can thank our Supreme Court justices for their liberal decisions regarding pornography that have contributed so significantly to this horrible condition.

The Entertainment Industry

Other dangers are more subtle. Consider television for example, or the Internet. Corporate entities as well as individuals are transmitting programming that violates every conceivable biblical standard of morality. Video and music stores provide tapes and CDs that contain images and lyrics that present a way of life that is terribly destructive. We can talk all we want about protecting children from "adult fare," but we cannot control every situation—including older siblings and other relatives as well as parents who violate biblical standards in their own lives.

Just recently, a young Christian couple was housesitting for some relatives. While perusing their video collection, they couldn't help but notice an explicit X-rated tape. Obviously, the couple that owned the house weren't particularly concerned that others knew that they were viewing movies that featured illicit and explicit sex. But this illustration leads to another very important principle that grows out of this Old Testament story.

Principle 2. Parents living in today's world must guard their own hearts and lives against the pagan influences that permeate our own culture.

This is a powerful principle that reflects the way Moses' parents did not allow the wickedness in Egypt and in their own

Israelite community to influence their lives. They maintained their faith in the God of Abraham, Isaac, and Jacob—and Joseph—in the midst of every sort of idolatry and immorality. Their example should give us hope, since most of us have advantages they didn't have. We're still surrounded with Christians who are committed to biblical standards of righteous behavior.

But we must be on guard. The evil influences of this world are everywhere. Furthermore, though Christian, we're still human. The lust and desires that make up the world are alluring and can easily ignite the desires of our own flesh that are out of harmony with God's perfect will. This is why the apostle John was so direct when he wrote to Christians living in the first-century world: "Do not love the world or anything in the world. If anyone loves the world, the love of the Father is not in him. For everything in the world—the cravings of sinful man, the lust of his eyes and the boasting of what he has and does—comes not from the Father but from the world. The world and its desires pass away, but the man who does the will of God lives forever" (1 John 2:15–17).

We must face reality. If we allow the world's system to press us into its mold as parents, we'll not protect our children from Satan's evil darts. They will become like us. Materialistic attitudes and actions beget materialistic attitudes and actions. Dishonesty begets dishonesty. A lukewarm approach to Christianity begets a lukewarm approach to Christianity—if not outright worldliness. Worst of all, hypocrisy—which our children can discern quickly—begets unbelief and rejection of the truth!

Principle 3. Christian parents living in today's world must take a proactive approach that is thoroughly biblical in order to protect their children from evil influences.

Here also we can learn a great lesson from Amram and Jochebed:

We, too, must trust God to help us be faithful parents. Good news! The Lord never asked us to face child-rearing problems in our own strength. We must believe God and trust Him to help us to be good parents. May it be said of us as people reflect back on our own lives: "*By faith,* these parents protected their children from the evil influences in this world!" (adapted from Heb. 11:23).

The Apostle Paul addressed this issue when he wrote to the Christians in Ephesus. First of all, he reminded them that their struggle was not "against flesh and blood, but against the rulers, against the authorities, against the powers of this dark world and against the spiritual forces of evil in the heavenly realms" (Eph. 6:12). Consequently, he instructed all Christians—which certainly includes Christian parents—to "put on the full armor of God," which he describes as "the belt of truth" and "the breastplate of righteousness." He also instructed them to have their "feet fitted with the readiness that comes from the gospel of peace." At this point, he stated: "In addition to all this, take up the *shield of faith,* with which you can extinguish all the flaming arrows of the evil one" (6:13–16).

We, too, must be courageous! Moses' parents were "not afraid" of Pharaoh's evil plans. Just so, we must not be afraid of "the devil's schemes." Our fear should be godly, which means we stand in awe of God and trust Him as our sovereign Creator. If this is our attitude, we need not fear Satan and his evil influences. Godly faith releases God's power in our lives— divine strength that will keep us from being paralyzed with fear. This is what Paul had in mind when he wrote to the Philippians: "Do not be anxious about anything, but in everything, by prayer and petition, with thanksgiving, present your requests to God. And the peace of God, which transcends all understanding, will guard your hearts and your minds in Christ Jesus" (Phil. 4:6–7).

We, too, must develop a strategy for protecting our children. Moses' parents did not simply trust God to protect their son.

Rather, they developed a unique plan especially suited to their particular crisis.

As Christian parents today, we cannot sit idly by, presuming on God's grace and allowing our Christian faith to be an escape from human responsibility. True, our faith should be foundational to all that we do—no matter what crises we face in our lives. But trusting God should not be an excuse for being passive.

Amram and Jochebed had a very detailed plan. I'm confident it was bathed in prayer. It was ingenious. They had done their own homework! They knew the exact time Pharaoh's daughter came to bathe. They knew the place Miriam could hide—and then suddenly appear at just the right moment. Miriam had certainly rehearsed her little speech many times. And certainly Jochebed had practiced again and again what she would say when the opportunity came.

Just so, as parents today, we must develop a specific strategy to protect our children from the evil in our present environment. That strategy must begin with consistency in our own lives. Modeling is a powerful means God has designed to help children develop an internal value system that will guide them in their decisions and actions the rest of their lives.

Principle 4. All Christian adults must join together in providing a safe, Christ-centered environment for our children.

It's true that Moses' parents probably faced this crisis alone. When the majority of their fellow Israelites had begun to worship the gods of Egypt, they had remained true to the God of Abraham, Isaac, and Jacob. What a tribute to Amram and Jochebed!

But it's also true that it's never been God's plan for the family unit to function in isolation and to face crises alone. This was true in the history of Israel, and as His redemptive plan continued to unfold, the Lord designed the church—the family of God—to provide a supportive environment for parents. Consequently, pastors, Sunday school teachers, youth leaders, and all members of Christ's body can and must join together in practicing the principles outlined in this chapter. All believers must be alert to the dangers in our society that are attempting to destroy our children. All of us as believers must guard our own hearts so we can become godly models. Furthermore, pastors and all church leaders should take a proactive, biblical approach that will provide activities that will support the family structure in nurturing children "in the training and instruction of the Lord" (Eph. 6:4).

Personalizing These Principles

1. How aware are you of the factors that exist in your community that are a threat to your own children—or grandchildren? Can you list these factors?

2. Are there any factors in your own life as a parent that may be keeping you from bringing your children up in the nurture and instruction of the Lord? Can you describe these factors?

3. What proactive approach are your taking to protect your children (or grandchildren) from the evil influences in your particular community? More specifically, how would you evaluate your faith in God—your ability to trust Him to protect your children? How would you describe your feelings about these matters? Are you fearful to the point that you cannot act rationally and responsibly? What specific strategy have you outlined either in your mind or on paper to bring up your children in the nurture and instruction of the Lord?

4. What is your church doing to support the family unit? How are you participating in this plan?

Set a Goal

In order to set a specific goal, reread the above questions and answer them as best you can. Be as specific as possible. As you do, ask the Holy Spirit to reveal to you the one thing you need to improve on the most. Based on this prayerful evaluation, set a specific goal to take corrective action:

_____

_____

_____

_____

Memorize the Following Scripture

Fathers, do not exasperate your children; instead, bring them up in the training and instruction of the Lord.
EPH. 6:4

Growing Together

The following questions are designed for small group discussion:

1. Would you share with us the factors in your own environment that you believe are the most threatening to our children or to our grandchildren?

2. What have you done specifically to model true Christian values to your children or your grandchildren? What changes would you like to make?

3. What practical steps have you taken in your family or church setting to protect your children from negative influences?

4. Would you feel free to share the personal goal you've set as a result of this study?

5. How can we pray for you specifically?

Chapter 2

A Life-changing Choice
Read Acts 7:20–22; Hebrews 11:24–26

I have a businessman friend who, prior to becoming a Christian, developed a very successful investment firm. He had carefully trained most of his employees, including his board of directors. But then he became a Christian. As he eagerly studied the Bible, he soon discovered he needed to make some significant changes in his lifestyle, and, as CEO of his company, he also knew he needed to make some changes in the way the company operated. Unfortunately, his board of directors—the men he had equipped for this position—didn't agree with his new value system. Because my friend owned only 40 percent of the company, they decided to fire him. One day he sat at the top of a very successful company, drawing a very substantial salary. The next day he was on the "outside looking in"!

Not only at that moment in his life but since then, my friend has made some tough choices to be a man of character in the business world. The choice we just described cost him his job—and his company! If he had it to do all over again, he would not compromise his convictions. In some respects, his experience reminds me of Moses' decision to identify with his own people—the children of Israel.

Moses was born during a time of great persecution. But in spite of the fact that his life could have been snuffed out at any moment, what appeared to be an unavoidable and heart-rending crisis turned into some unusual advantages for Moses. Both his heredity and environment blended in a unique way to set him apart, first among the Egyptians and then among his own people.

Advantages and Achievements

As a young man growing up, Moses had very little to do with his heritage and his opportunities for achievement. All he had to do was to take advantage of these opportunities and turn them into accomplishments.

Once again, the New Testament gives us some unusual insights into Moses' early life. Stephen, in his dynamic message in the book of Acts, points out that Moses had outstanding physical assets, unusual intellectual abilities, and exceptional leadership skills. Note the following: "At that time Moses was born, and he was *no ordinary child.* For three months he was cared for in his father's house. When he was placed outside, Pharaoh's daughter took him and brought him up as her own son. Moses was educated in *all the wisdom of the Egyptians* and was *powerful in speech and action*" (Acts 7:20–22).

The Future "Mr. Egypt"

The Greek word Stephen used to describe Moses can be translated "fair," "beautiful," or "handsome." He was definitely referring to Moses' physical traits. In this sense, he was "no ordinary child" (NIV). From the moment Moses was born, he was a striking specimen of humanity. In the Old Testament account, we read that Jochebed "saw that he was a *fine* child" (Exod. 2:2)—the word translated "fine" can also be translated "beautiful." In the New Testament, the author of the book of Hebrews included both parents in this tribute. Both Amram and Jochebed recognized that Moses was "no ordinary child" (Heb. 11:23).

It's true that "man looks at the outward appearance, but the LORD looks at the heart" (1 Sam. 16:7). From God's perspective, inner qualities are more important than external qualities. However, Moses had both. From the moment he was born, he was eligible to be an outstanding candidate for winning both the "Mr. Egypt" and the "Mr. Israel" awards.

The Jewish historian Josephus gives us another interesting insight. As Moses grew to manhood, he had such outstanding physical features that the Egyptians looked for the opportunity to simply catch a glimpse of him as he walked by or floated down the river on his golden barge. Some who were privileged to "take a long look," would often stare at him, finding it hard to turn their eyes away from this unusual young man. Since Moses was also known as the "son of Pharaoh's daughter" and the apparent heir to the king's throne, this simply added to the intrigue people sensed when they knew he was nearby.

A Brilliant Scholar

When Moses eventually left his Jewish home (probably at about age four or five) and went to live in the king's court, he began an educational career that was second to none in the pagan world. As Stephen stated, he "was educated in all the wisdom of the Egyptians" (Acts 7:22). Moses became a scholar. Today he would at least have a "Ph.D." behind his name—if not several doctoral degrees.

Remember, too, that at this moment in history, Egypt represented one of the most productive and progressive countries in the world. The nation's social, economic, and educational achievements were almost unprecedented. To this day, the pyramids stand as a tribute to the almost unbelievable achievements of the Egyptian architects and builders. These fascinating structures reflect mathematical insights, artistic skills, and feats of engineering that are almost inconceivable for a culture that existed so many years ago.

Think for a moment what this means! Moses was probably the most educated young man in all of Egypt—if not in the world of his day. Who would have had a greater opportunity than the son of Pharaoh's daughter—the young man who lived in the king's palace as a part of the royal family and who had access to every educational resource and opportunity Egypt could offer? He had free tuition, personalized instruction from the best scholars in the land, and an eager, inquiring young mind. Moses was destined to graduate from the "University of Egypt" *summa cum laude.*

A Man for All Seasons

Moses was not just a theoretician—a man who could fascinate other scholars by working out complicated mathematical formulas or by spicing up his lectures by using several foreign languages. Rather, he translated his intellectual achievements into life. As Stephen stated, Moses "was powerful in speech and *action*" (Acts 7:22b).

This means that Moses became an outstanding educator himself. What he knew, he communicated to others. He had power with words—a skill that enabled him to command respect and to direct and lead people.

Josephus gives us an additional insight regarding Moses' leadership abilities. When the Ethiopians attacked Egypt and were on the verge of defeating them, the Pharaoh appointed Moses as general over the Egyptian army. Under his dynamic leadership, the Ethiopians were driven back and defeated. Perhaps this is what the Holy Spirit was referring to when He inspired Stephen to utter that Moses "was powerful in" both "speech and action" (Acts 7:22b).

Tough Choices

At some point in life, Moses began to understand that there was more to life than being the center of attention and rising to a place of prominence in Egypt. His early childhood memories of his own parents' home probably never faded. He certainly remembered some of the hardships his family had faced because of Egyptian slavery and bondage. And in spite of his pagan upbringing in the Pharaoh's court, he must have remembered that his parents had faith in one they identified as the God of Israel.

As Moses traveled about the land, riding in a golden chariot or cruising up and down the Nile in the king's private barge, what he saw evidently kept his childhood memories alive. He saw the same slavery and brutal treatment. But where was the faith in the God of Abraham, Isaac, and Jacob he had seen in his parents? Even the Israelites were worshiping the gods of Egypt. Why weren't they worshiping the God who had delivered him from a watery grave?

We're not told when these thoughts began to grip Moses. Perhaps his inquiring mind and educational background motivated him to study his own heritage. It's possible he secretly made his way to his parents' humble home and talked to them about his national and religious background. Or God may have actually spoken directly to Moses.

One thing is certain: Moses became aware of his Hebrew heritage. He discovered that God had a special plan for his life and for His people—a plan that was diametrically opposed to the one that was unfolding in the mind of his foster mother.

Again, we're not told how long Moses struggled with the tension he was feeling inside. But eventually, he came to the place where he made some decisions—tough decisions! He knew he had to choose either to identify with his own people and experience unusual suffering or to maintain his identity with royalty and experience all the things the world had to offer. To choose to identify with his fellow Israelites would lead to an eternal reward. To choose to remain as an Egyptian leader would only give him earthly benefits.

The author of Hebrews makes it very clear which decisions Moses made:

- By faith Moses, when he had grown up, refused to be known as the son of Pharaoh's daughter (Heb. 11:24).
- He chose to be mistreated along with the people of God rather than to enjoy the pleasures of sin for a short time (11:25).
- He regarded disgrace for the sake of Christ as of greater value than the treasures of Egypt, because he was looking ahead to his reward (11:26).

Slavery Versus Royalty

Moses must have spent many agonizing days counting the cost that would accompany his decision to identify with his own people. Since he was a very sensitive man, he would be deeply concerned about his foster mother. She had saved his life. She had provided him with all the advantages of an Egyptian education. She had given him the opportunity to become a great leader in Egypt. In fact, what she had provided him would make it possible for him to become an heir to the throne of Egypt.

Imagine the emotional agony he must have experienced when he announced to her one day that he no longer could be called her son. On the one hand, she must have shed bitter tears because of the rejection she felt. On the other hand, she may have lashed out at Moses with bitter words, accusing him of being ungrateful and insensitive.

This decision would also result in great personal sacrifice. Moses chose to leave a position of prominence to become a "nobody." He chose to leave a place of acceptance and honor for one of rejection and dishonor. He chose to leave fame and fortune to become a servant without any personal resources.

When all was said and done, however, Moses knew he had no choice—if he wanted to be in the will of God. He had to identify with his own people. He had to reject his royal position. Difficult as it was, Moses chose to identify with slavery rather than royalty.

Suffering Versus Pleasure

Moses' choice meant both emotional rejection and physical suffering. This choice meant being "mistreated along with the people of God" rather than enjoying "the pleasures of sin for a short time" (Heb. 11:25).

The "pleasures of sin" that Moses gave up certainly refers to more than the personal enjoyment that we experience when we indulge our sensual appetites. The "pleasures" he gave up included the satisfaction he would have felt if he had continued his identity with Egypt rather than Israel. The "pleasures" certainly involved choosing an easy road rather than a difficult road identifying with slavery. Moses chose the difficult path— the path of persecution and pain. But in making this choice, he also experienced the positive emotions that accompany a decision "to obey God rather than man"—a deep, settled peace and joy in the midst of suffering.

Spiritual Rewards Versus Earthly Rewards

Moses was already a very wealthy man. From the time he had gone to live in Pharaoh's court, he had everything materially anyone could ever want. He wore royal garments made from exquisite fabrics. He ate the best food Egypt could offer. He had an open ended allowance. Servants attended his every need. And, if he had remained in the royal court, Moses would eventually have had access to all the wealth of Egypt.

Moses saw beyond the temporal and the material. He "regarded disgrace for the sake of Christ as of greater value than the treasures of Egypt, because he was looking ahead to his reward" (11:26). With the eye of faith, he saw an eternal reward—a reward that would never fade away. And even though his decision meant rejection, poverty, and suffering,

Moses was willing to pay the price to inherit this eternal reward.

Isn't it fascinating that the author of Hebrews made reference to Jesus Christ? This is particularly significant since Moses knew little, if anything, about the coming Messiah. What is even more enlightening is that his decision illustrates the choice Jesus Christ made when He willingly left His royal position in heaven to become a mere man and a servant and to suffer death on the cross.

Moses did not understand all that was happening in his life, but his heavenly Father did. And millennia later, we have the unique and wonderful privilege of understanding this choice and how God viewed it. We now know that Moses responded to the light he had, and when he did, he entered the Hebrews "Hall of Faith" along with other Old Testament greats. In fact, he was destined to become one of the greatest Old Testament prophets who ever lived (Deut. 34:10–12).

Becoming God's Man Today

Principles to Live By

Very few of us will ever be able to identify with Moses in terms of his physical assets, his intellectual accomplishments, and his leadership abilities. Furthermore, we'll never be able to identify directly with the circumstances that caused him to make the decisions he knew in his heart he had to make. But even though the literal aspects of Moses' decisions are unusual, there are some very practical principles that flow from his choices that spell out God's will for us today.

Principle 1. God wants all of us as His children to use fully the time, talent, and treasures He has given each one of us in order to bring glory to His name.

Moses is unique in biblical history. He had unusual physical assets from birth and his I.Q. was off the charts! Furthermore, he had incredible social and cultural opportunities to develop his natural capabilities. He never lacked the financial and people resources to achieve his educational goals. Consequently, God expected a lot more from Moses than He did from other people in Israel, including their leaders.

This principle applies to all of us today. God has provided each of us with certain capabilities and opportunities. He is aware, of course, of our environmental obstacles and road-blocks—for example, the problems we have faced in our family life. He knows our inherent weaknesses and the circumstances that are beyond our control. But at the same time, God wants us to use what we have at our disposal. He wants us to develop our capacities and use them to the fullest.

Our Time and Talents

Jesus made this point very clear one day when He was teaching His disciples: "From everyone who has been given much, much will be demanded; and from the one who has been entrusted with much, much more will be asked" (Luke 12:48b).

Jesus Christ was referring to many aspects of our lives.

- If He has given us an outgoing personality, He expects us to use that ability to honor the Lord and to attract people to Jesus Christ.
- If He has given us great intellectual abilities, He expects us to use these capacities to learn all we can and to use that information to carry out His purpose in the world.
- If we have grown up in a home that has been safe and secure, He expects us to use our own sense of security to reach out to others who are less fortunate and help them develop feelings of safety and protection within the family of God.
- If we've inherited or been able to make large amounts of money, He expects us to use our material resources generously to further the work of His kingdom.

- If He is giving us an opportunity at this moment to get an education, He expects us to learn all we can in that environment and not waste time and effort.
- If we've already obtained a great education, He expects us to use our educational experience to carry out His goals in this world.
- If He has given us unusual talents and abilities, God expects us to use those talents and abilities to carry out the Great Commission.
- If He has given us a wonderful wife and children, He expects us to do all we can to provide for them, but also to model what it means to be a true man of character.

Our Treasures

Materialism was often a great stumbling block in Jesus' day—and it is today! In fact, on one occasion, a very wealthy young man came to Him and asked Him what he must do to inherit eternal life. Jesus told him in unequivocal terms that he should sell all that he had and give it to the poor. However, because this man was very rich, he sadly turned and walked away (Matt. 19:16–22).

What Jesus said that day has caused some people to also "turn and walk away." They don't stay around long enough to find out what Jesus was really teaching. No one can inherit eternal life by selling everything and giving it away. In fact, no one can be saved except by grace through faith—not works (Eph. 2:8–9).

The man that came to Jesus that day missed the point completely. If he had truly been interested in eternal life, if he were truly interested in putting God first, if he really were interested in knowing who Jesus was—he would have gladly pursued the conversation further. But Jesus knew his real problem because He knew what was in his heart. Wealth was far more important to this young man than spiritual things.

Jesus also knew that anything He would say would not change
the young man's mind. Consequently, Jesus zeroed in on his
weakness and unveiled his heart and his motives. The Lord
wasted no time going directly to the "bottom line"—in this
case, this man's materialistic "god."

Applied to a born-again Christian, Jesus was dealing with
our priorities. He wants all of us to "seek first his kingdom
and his righteousness," and trust God that "all these things
will be given to [us] as well" (Matt. 6:33).

Principle 2. God wants all of us as His children to make choices that will enable us to live in His perfect will.

Few of us will ever be asked to make the literal choices Moses
had to make. In fact, most of us will never be asked to make
the decisions Jesus asked of the twelve apostles. Like Moses,
they had a very special calling. On the other hand, God
wants all of us to make choices that always put Him first in
our lives.

To follow Jesus fully *does* mean that we'll need to make
choices that often lead to sacrifice. There *are* the "pleasures of
sin" that have no part in a Christian's experience. In this sense,
we cannot "have our cake and eat it too"—unless we want to
experience some unusual tension and discipline in our lives. If
we are truly God's children and not illegitimate, our heavenly
Father will ultimately deal with our sins—not because He
takes pleasure in hurting us but because He loves us and
knows what's best for us! (Heb. 12:7–11).

As we've seen, to follow Jesus fully means to "seek first his
kingdom and his righteousness," realizing that the things we
need to live "will be given to [us] as well" (Matt. 6:33).
Though we may never be asked to give up a beautiful palace
or a significant material inheritance, God does want us to use
these provisions first and foremost to glorify Him. We must
never put material possessions before God. There is no place
for materialism in a dedicated Christian's life.

To follow Jesus fully may mean suffering rejection from our parents. They may not be Christians—and they may not understand our commitment to Christ. In fact, on one occasion, Jesus turned and spoke to the large crowds that were following Him: "If anyone comes to me and does not hate his father and mother, his wife and children, his brothers and sisters—yes, even his own life—he cannot be my disciple. And anyone who does not carry his cross and follow me cannot be my disciple" (Luke 14:25–26).

Some people have stumbled over this statement—just like the rich young man misunderstood Jesus' challenge to sell everything and follow Him in order to be saved. First of all, Jesus Christ was not justifying "hate," which He so specifically condemned in the Sermon on the Mount (Matt. 5:43–48). Neither was He justifying parental neglect. He condemned the Pharisees for devising a system that would classify their material possessions as being "devoted to God" so they wouldn't have to take care of their aging fathers and mothers. This was a direct violation of God's command to "honor" our "father and mother" (Matt. 15:5–6; Exod. 20:12). And who can forget what Jesus did when He was hanging on the cross and turned to His beloved friend, John, and asked him to take care of His own mother (John 19:25–27)?

What Jesus *was* saying is that not one of us can really follow Him fully if others are more important than He is. We must love God first and foremost. All others in our lives must be second— including our wives, our children, our brothers and sisters in Christ, and our friends. When we put God first, all of these other relationships will come into proper focus. Our priorities will then be in order. It must be God first and family second.

Even Coach Vince Lombardi understood this principle. One of the reasons he led the Green Bay Packers to do great exploits on the gridiron was that he instilled in his team members a very important sequence. Bart Starr, quarterback for the Packers, said this of his coach: "He always said there were three central things in life, in order of priority: Number 1, religion; Number 2, family; Number 3, the Green Bay Packers."[1] This order of priority motivated Lombardi's players to do their best in their chosen vocation—and to be winners.

Principle 3. God wants all of His children to walk through life seeing beyond the temporal and on into eternity.

In this sense, Old Testament greats teach us a wonderful lesson. They definitely saw beyond life on this earth. When Moses made his decision to identify with his people, he was motivated by eternal values. Abraham also followed God fully because "he was looking forward to the city with foundations whose architect and builder is God" (Heb. 11:10). The author of Hebrews summarizes this idea by referring to a number of those listed in this great Hebrew "Hall of Faith": "All these people were still living by faith when they died. They did not receive the things promised; they only saw them and welcomed them from a distance. And they admitted that they were aliens and strangers on earth. People who say such things show that they are looking for a country of their own. If they had been thinking of the country they had left, they would have had opportunity to return. *Instead, they were longing for a better country—a heavenly one"* (Heb. 11:13–16a).

Unfortunately, many Christians today lose sight of the fact that our real citizenship is in heaven. We are indeed strangers and aliens on earth. In the words of the old gospel song— "This world is not my home, I'm just passing through."

God has left us on earth to fulfill His purposes—to bring glory to His name by building His kingdom. This means being devoted to carrying out the Great Commission. We are to be busy at this great task—both directly and indirectly— until Jesus Christ comes again. Some of us will be more directly involved by "going" and winning people to Christ and planting churches. Others of us will be more indirectly involved through giving and praying for those who are more directly involved. But all of us together are carrying out the real reason we have been left on earth.

Personalizing These Principles

1. To what extent are you using to the full the time, talents, and treasures God has given you to bring glory to His name?

   A Caution: This question is not designed to put you on a guilt trip. Some Christians are very sensitive and feel they *never* measure up to what God expects. If you're having difficulty answering this question, consult several other believers in Christ that you respect and admire and who are known for their wisdom and balanced approach to living the Christian life, and ask them to help you evaluate your lifestyle.

2. To what extent are you making choices that are enabling you to live in God's perfect will?

   A Challenge: After meditating on Romans 12:1–2, highlight every directive that Paul included in the rest of this letter (Rom. 12–16). Then use these directives as a basis for evaluating whether or not you are making decisions that are within God's perfect will.

3. To what extent are you walking through life with eternity's values in view?

   A Charge: This does not mean we do not have very important responsibilities that need to be carried out from day to day. It's God's will that we work and earn a living. For example, some of the Thessalonian Christians used the truth regarding Christ's Second Coming to be lazy and to take advantage of other Christians. Paul set the record straight and charged the Christians in this church to correct this problem: "For even when we were with you, we gave you this rule: 'If a man will not work, he shall not eat'" (2 Thess. 3:10).

Set a Goal

As you reflect on the principles in this chapter, what area needs the most attention? Once the Holy Spirit reveals this to you, set a personal goal:

———————————————————————

———————————————————————

———————————————————————

———————————————————————

Memorize the Following Scripture

But seek first his kingdom and his righteousness, and all these things will be given to you as well.
MATT. 6:33

Growing Together

1. How are you using the opportunities God has given you to glorify Him? What opportunities have you missed? What opportunities would you like to use more fully? Do you feel good about the way you are using your time? Your talents? Your treasures?

2. How do you determine what choices to make in life? What choices have you made you wish you hadn't? How could you have avoided making these choices? If you had these choices to make over again, what choices would you make?

3. How do we maintain a balance between keeping our eyes on eternal values and carrying out our day-to-day

responsibilities—on the job, in our families, and in our churches? Would you be able to share an area in your life where you feel you have gotten off balance? How did you correct this imbalance?

4. How can we pray for you specifically?

Chapter 3

A Sincere but Self-centered Decision

Read Exodus 2:11–15; Acts 7:23–29

*I*s it possible to be sincere but self-centered at the same time? As men, we face this temptation all the time. After all, we live in a culture that promotes self-reliance and the importance of being self-confident. It's easy to buy into this philosophy of life, yet be sincere. We believe this is the right way to live—that it's even God's way!

What makes this error so subtle is that "being self-confident" and "believing in ourselves" is not wrong in itself. In fact, it is a very necessary ingredient in being successful—in most everything we do. Many men have failed in business, as leaders in their families, and as church members because they lack self-confidence. But there's a difference between being "self-confident" and "self-centered." Moses had to learn this lesson the hard way!

A Sacrificial Choice

At this point in our story, Moses has already chosen to identify with his own people and their difficult plight rather than to be a part of the king's family and enjoy the earthly benefits of royalty. We're not told how he became aware of God's specific plan for his life. Perhaps his parents shared this divine perspective when he slipped away from the palace and visited their little slave hut.

But how would Moses' parents know what God had in mind for their little boy? Josephus reports that God had appeared in a dream to Amram, Moses' father, and revealed His plan for Moses. Even though this incident is not a part of the biblical record, it's conceivable that it happened. Let's not forget that God revealed Himself through an angel to both Zacharias and Mary and told them of the birth and destiny of both John the Baptist and Jesus Christ. If the Lord had revealed this truth to Moses' parents in some divine way, it helps explain their faith and trust in God when Pharaoh issued his edict that all newborn boys should be thrown into the Nile.

But one thing is certain. In some way, Moses had discovered that God had chosen him to deliver the children of Israel from slavery and bondage. Once he understood this divine calling and made his decision to give himself sacrificially to his people, he was ready to move into action. This shouldn't surprise us. From what we know about his God-given talents and Egyptian education, he had become a "Mr. Charge Ahead"-type personality.

But in spite of Moses' great achievements and even his ability to command armies, he wasn't ready to carry out God's special plan for his life—even though he had been "educated in all the wisdom of the Egyptians and was powerful in speech and action" (Acts 7:22). These talents did not qualify him to handle the gigantic responsibility that lay ahead of him. Moses had yet to learn that God's work must be done in God's way and in God's time. It would take him another forty years to learn this lesson. Like so many of us, Moses had to make some serious mistakes before he understood God's specific will for his life.

The Power of Negative Experiences

One day one of my elders in the church I pastor approached me and somewhat shocked me. "Gene," he said, "one of your greatest strengths is trusting people. However," he continued, "one of your greatest weaknesses is trusting people you shouldn't trust."

Well, you guessed it! He had a reason to make this observation. It was true. I had trusted some people I shouldn't have—and it backfired on me, creating some real problems in the church. Since then, I haven't lost my trusting nature, and I hope I never will. But I've also learned to seek more wisdom from others in making judgments about people. Hopefully, I'll never forget this lesson. It was a negative experience, but one I needed to teach me a lesson I would not have learned otherwise.

God knows that we often learn best through negative experiences. In fact, this seems to be the only way we can learn some lessons. This is not to say that we don't need success. This too is a great teacher. In fact, nothing succeeds like success! But, when our success is unbroken by failure, we can become overly dependent on our own capabilities.

Up to this time in his life, Moses had experienced nothing but success. He had been miraculously delivered from death while many other babies his own age had been brutally killed. Suddenly, he had become a member of the royal family and was protected by the evil Pharaoh's own daughter. Ironically, she arranged for Moses' own mother to care for him during the early years of his life, providing him with a deep sense of security. Once he went to live in the king's palace, he had unparalleled educational opportunities. Everyone in Egypt admired him—including the king. He could do no wrong! Consequently, he had a great self-image! He definitely "believed" in Moses!

This was not wrong in itself. However, at this point in his life, Moses approached challenges the only way he knew how—with faith in his own strength and abilities. This does not mean he didn't believe in God and the importance of having a spiritual perspective on life. In fact, this is what motivated him to decide to identify with his own people. But his theology was more man-centered than God-centered. This is why the Lord introduced him to His "wilderness school"—a "series of courses" that would take forty years to complete!

Parallel Passages

Following are two biblical accounts of what happened next in Moses' life. One is from the Old Testament and the second from the New Testament. Together, these passages provide us with some fascinating insights into Moses' personality.

A Sense of Justice

Exodus 2:11–12	Acts 7:23–25
One day, after Moses had grown up, he went out to where his own people were and watched them at their hard labor. He saw an Egyptian beating a Hebrew, one of his own people. Glancing this way and that and seeing no one, he killed the Egyptian and hid him in the sand.	When Moses was forty years old, he decided to visit his fellow Israelites. He saw one of them being mistreated by an Egyptian, so he went to his defense and avenged him by killing the Egyptian. Moses thought that his own people would realize that God was using him to rescue them, but they did not.

Once Moses decided to sever his relationships with the royal family, he began to pay attention to what was happening in the lives of his own people. As he walked through the fields, the first thing that hit him full force was the way his fellow Israelites were being treated. On one occasion, he saw an Egyptian unmercifully beating a fellow Hebrew. Though he had probably seen this happen before, he felt compelled to act on this injustice. Anger stirred in his soul. Looking in all directions, he pounced on the Egyptian. With brute strength and skill, he landed a blow that killed this taskmaster—a move he no doubt learned in the king's court at the hands of some of the most skilled fighters in the land of Egypt.

After Moses had attempted to hide what he had done from the Egyptian taskmasters, perhaps he had hoped that the word would spread among his own people—"The deliverer has come! The deliverer has come!" But he was in for a rude awakening! Word definitely spread—but not the way he had hoped. Moses did not anticipate that his fellow Israelites would not accept him as their deliverer and then leak the story back to the Egyptians. This is clear from what happened next.

Intense Rejection

Exodus 2:13–14a	Acts 7:26–27
The next day he went out and saw two Hebrews fighting. He asked the one in the wrong, "Why are you hitting your fellow Hebrew?" The man said, "Who made you ruler and judge over us?"	The next day Moses came upon two Israelites who were fighting. He tried to reconcile them by saying, "Men, you are brothers; why do you want to hurt each other?" But the man who was mistreating the other *pushed Moses aside* and said, "Who made you ruler and judge over us?"

This must have been a shattering experience for Moses. Perhaps no one had ever laid a hand on him—let alone pushed him away! To add insult to injury, one of the men he was trying to help rejected him verbally by saying, "Who made you ruler and judge over us?" (Acts 7:27).

Try to identify with what Moses must have felt at that moment. He had just made one of the most sacrificial decisions that any man could make. As royalty, he had chosen to identify with his own people and with their suffering. This meant giving up the glories of Egyptian cultural splendor. It meant giving up his position as the son of the king's daughter. It meant laying aside the prospect of becoming the future king of Egypt. And to prove the sincerity of his heart, he laid his own life on the line for an Israelite the day before.

A Serious Misunderstanding

Exodus 2:14b–15	Acts 7:28–29
"Are you thinking of killing me as you killed the Egyptian?" Then Moses was afraid and thought, "What I did must have become known." When Pharaoh heard of this, he tried to kill Moses, but Moses fled from Pharaoh and went to live in Midian, where he sat down by a well.	"Do you want to kill me as you killed the Egyptian yesterday?" When Moses heard this, he fled to Midian, where he settled as a foreigner and had two sons.

It's one thing to be rejected for doing something you think is right, but it is yet another thing to have your motives completely misunderstood. But this was just the beginning of Moses' problems. When Pharaoh heard what had happened, he put out an all-points alert, not only to capture the "future king of Egypt," but to have him executed.

Moses' boldness suddenly turned to fear. His self-confidence dropped to zero. He knew he was in serious trouble. The news of what he had done spread like wildfire, not just among the children of Israel but among the Egyptians.

A Horrendous "Catch-22"

Moses faced a dilemma few men ever face. He had already told Pharaoh's daughter that he was severing his relationship with royalty. The Pharaoh had to be terribly angry over what he would conceive as inexcusable ingratitude and betrayal. But even if the door had been left open for Moses to reconsider his decision, what he had now done eliminated all possibilities. He had just burned every bridge behind him. His position in Egypt was gone forever.

He was also unwelcome among his own people. They would never harbor a murderer who could bring the wrath of the king down on them in an even greater measure. Furthermore, they did not understand that Moses was chosen by God to be their savior.

Moses had only one choice. He had to run for his life! His royal career was over. And all of his good intentions with his own people had backfired.

As Moses was trudging across the desert, he must have concluded that he had made a serious mistake! As far as we know, the God he had given up everything to serve may have actually "ceased to exist" in his mind and heart. It would not be surprising since disillusionment always brings doubt.

Penetrating Insights

As we reflect on what has just happened in Moses' life, we can understand more clearly what caused his bad judgments:

His motivation was primarily emotional rather than rational. When Moses saw the Egyptian taskmaster physically abusing one of his brothers, he became very angry. Obviously, he was moved with compassion and felt sorry for his fellow Israelite. At that moment his "heart" got ahead of his "head." Rather than controlling his emotions and continuing on his fact-finding mission, he lost his temper and became involved with a single incident that led to an irrational act—murder—that destroyed respect for him among the Egyptians and blew away any opportunity to gain respect from his own people.

Even so, God—who knows the end from the beginning—was preparing Moses for a *future task*. He knew Moses' heart and his tendency to become emotional. But God also knew that the task He had designed for Moses would call for a motivational perspective that would carry him through the good times and the tough times. Moses was not yet ready for this task. His educational background in Egypt—even though he was forty years old—had not prepared him adequately. Unknown to Moses, it would take another forty years to get ready to carry out the task God had for him.

Moses was operating in his own strength. Moses' actions were based on his own strength rather than on God's power. Obviously, he was a very well-built and strong man, and you can be sure that during his early life, he often used this strength to his advantage. Even after he fled from Egypt and went to the land of Midian, one of the first things he did was to confront some shepherds who were harassing several women at a desert well (Exod. 2:16–29). Singlehandedly, he drove them away.

All during Moses' early life, he had been admired for his physical abilities. And at this moment, when he believed that he was destined to become Israel's deliverer, he fell back upon the only thing he really knew how to use in this kind of crisis —his brute strength.

Moses had to learn that God's victories are usually not won in ordinary ways. His strategies for defeating the Ethiopians as the leader of the Egyptian army would not work in this case. God's divine plan for ushering the children of Israel out of Egypt and caring for them in the wilderness was going to call for power beyond anything Moses had ever witnessed or dreamed of.

Moses eventually learned this lesson. After the Lord miraculously and with His mighty power delivered the children of Israel from the Egyptian army by parting the waters of the Red Sea, he sang out with glorious exaltation: "*Your right hand, O LORD, was majestic in power.* Your right hand, O LORD, shattered the enemy. In the greatness of your majesty you threw down those who opposed you. You unleashed your burning anger; it consumed them like stubble" (Exod. 15:6–7).

When Moses took it upon himself to be the deliverer, he used his own strength and struck down an Egyptian and killed him—perhaps with his "own right hand." However, forty years later, God in His own anger struck down thousands with His "right hand"! He used Moses as a human instrument but only to raise his staff and stretch out his "hand over the sea" (14:16). It was God's power that divided the waters so the Israelites could pass over on dry ground.

Moses' mistake caused his rejection. Not all rejection is caused by making mistakes. Consider Jesus Christ, who was rejected by His own people (John 1:11). Later, Moses would experience rejection again and again from "his own people" as they traveled from Egypt to Canaan—not because he made a lot of mistakes but because he was doing the will of God. However, when he was first rejected by his own people as well as the Egyptians, it was because he made several serious errors in judgment.

First, Moses miscalculated the response he would get from the children of Israel. Because he had grown up as the center of attention in Egypt and as a very successful leader, he concluded he would be "welcomed" by his own people—a conclusion which is not surprising. Egocentric people generally seem to have this false perception. Moses was no exception. Consequently, when he heard the words "Who made you ruler and judge over us?" he was devastated, particularly in view of his pure motives and sincere efforts.

Second, Moses made a serious mistake when he lost his temper and lost control. The Israelite, and perhaps others, who saw him kill the Egyptian also saw him look in every direction. They must have seen the fear on his face and his secretive behavior. They no doubt sensed his lack of perspective on the total situation; for no man who has wisdom and good sense would try to deliver the children of Israel by attacking men one on one. It would take a far more comprehensive strategy and plan. Consequently, this serious error in judgment served to destroy any confidence the Israelites needed in order to put their faith in Moses.

Becoming God's Man Today

Principles to Live By

No man living today can identify totally with Moses' life and ministry. His calling was unique and his task unequaled. Outside of Christ Himself, no man had a greater challenge calling for unusual preparation and endurance. Yet all of us can identify with certain aspects of his life, which yield some dynamic principles that we can apply to our lives every day.

Principle 1. Decisions that are more emotional than rational often get us into serious difficulties.

Motivation that is based on a rational approach to life is enduring. When we take a rational approach to problem solving, we're looking through God's eyes. When we take an approach to problem solving that is primarily emotional, we're looking through our own eyes. Obviously, God is both rational and emotional, but He makes decisions based upon clear thinking.

On the other hand, emotional decisions are usually short-lived. As long as we "feel" good, we perform. When we slide off the other side of the mountain, we find ourselves in the valley and unable to carry out the goals we set for ourselves at the time we were experiencing an emotional high.

Motivation that is based on a rational approach to decision making and action is the only kind of motivation that will carry us through the vicissitudes of life. It is this kind of motivation, "prepared in season and out of season" (2 Tim. 4:2), that acts when we "feel" like it and when we don't. It is this kind of motivation that enabled Jesus Christ to continue on His way to the cross, when in the garden He prayed, "My Father, if it is possible, may this cup be taken from me. Yet not as I will, but as You will" (Matt. 26:39). Today God needs men who will not turn back, who will keep on carrying out the will of God, no matter what the circumstances or problems in life.

Principle 2. God wants us to tackle challenges in His strength but at the same time, to use all of our talents and abilities.

It does take human effort to do God's work. We are not robots that operate on "supernatural batteries." We must always remember that God's work is God's work, and we must never allow ourselves to think that we can take matters into our own hands. Writing to the Ephesians, Paul said, "Finally, be strong in the Lord and in his mighty power. Put on the full armor of God so that you can take your stand against the devil's schemes" (Eph. 6:10–11).

A careful study of this armor will show there is a unique and significant balance between human effort and reliance upon God. We are basically responsible to have our loins girded with truth, to put on the breastplate of righteousness, and to shod our feet with the Gospel of peace. This takes God's grace, yet it is our human responsibility. But it is *faith*, *salvation* (our position in Christ), the *Word of God*, and *prayer*—all divine resources—that unlock the resources of heaven. Christians must always maintain this balance if they are going to be effective in God's work. But remember, God's strength and power are always foundational. Without Him, we can do nothing that will last and endure.

Principle 3. All Christians will experience rejection for doing the will of God, but often we are rejected because of our own foolish mistakes.

Some Christians have the mistaken notion that there is blessing and reward in being persecuted per se. Consequently, they set out to make people angry and set themselves up for rejection.

Unfortunately, this happened among certain groups who were victims of communist oppression. They became the underground church, which had a certain legitimacy at a particular time. The persecution eventually subsided. However, some

Christians had developed a "persecution mentality" and went out of their way to aggravate the government. Furthermore, they continued to "meet in secret" when they no longer had to go underground.

Paul was often persecuted for preaching the Gospel. But he never taught Christians to make persecution their goal. Rather, he wrote to the Romans and said, "If it is possible, as far as it depends on you, live at peace with everyone" (Rom. 12:18). Note also what Paul instructed Timothy to do when he was ministering in Ephesus: "I urge, then, first of all, that requests, prayers, intercession and thanksgiving be made for everyone—for kings and all those in authority, that we may live peaceful and quiet lives in all godliness and holiness. This is good, and pleases God our Savior, who wants all men to be saved and to come to a knowledge of the truth" (1 Tim. 2:1–4).

To suffer for righteousness' sake is praiseworthy, but to suffer because we've done something foolish is what we deserve. How easy it is to defend ourselves even when we've made a serious error! How easy it is to put the blame on someone else! If we've made a mistake we must admit it, correct the situation (if we can), learn from it, and then proceed to live a more mature and responsible life.

Personalizing These Principles

Honestly ask yourself which of the following problems you have faced the most in your life. Check the one you feel applies to you:

❑ Being motivated more by emotion than reason.

❑ Trying to do God's work in my own strength alone.

❑ Suffering rejection because of my own mistakes.

Think. How could you have acted differently?

Pray. Ask God to help you face life's situations in a more mature and responsible way.

Set a Goal

As you reflect on the principles outlined in this chapter, what one goal do you need to set for your life?

_____

_____

_____

_____

Memorize the Following Scripture

If any of you lacks wisdom, he should ask God, who gives generously to all without finding fault, and it will be given to him.
JAMES 1:5

Growing Together

1. How have you learned to apply the principles outlined in this chapter in your own life?

2. Would you feel free to share what principle you feel you have violated the most and how you would like to better apply the principle?

3. Would you feel free to share what happened when you violated a particular principle? How did the other people involved react? In turn, how did you react?

4. How can we pray for you specifically?

Chapter 4

The Immobilizing Power of an Inferiority Complex

Read Exodus 2:15–25; 3:1–22; 4:1–20

All of us can remember negative experiences that have marked us to this very day. Psychologists call these "traumatic experiences"—events in our lives that have left emotional wounds. The most common results are feelings of inferiority and insecurity.

Moses had this kind of intense emotional and spiritual experience. After what must have been months—or perhaps even years—searching his own soul, he decided to give up the glories of Egypt to identify with his own people. He chose to suffer with the people of God rather than enjoy all the "pleasures of sin" that were available in Egypt. But while attempting to carry out his decisions, Moses was broadsided with rejection by both the children of Israel and the Egyptians.

Moses faced a terrible dilemma. He had nowhere to turn except to flee into the wilderness, a rejected and dejected man. Like most men who appear invincible, underneath his strong, self-confident, and handsome exterior, Moses was a very sensitive individual. In fact, he was so sensitive that he was affected by this rejection for the next forty years.

"In the Fullness of Time"

In his zeal to deliver Israel from Egyptian bondage, Moses took matters into his own hands. He totally miscalculated God's timing. This was a serious mistake. But God did not forget Israel—or Moses. He was definitely God's man, the one the Lord had chosen to lead Israel out of Egypt. Sometimes we may think that God is deaf and doesn't care, but in His own time He responds. He did this for Israel (Exod. 2:23–3:10).

Eventually, the wicked Pharaoh died. Even so, his successor promoted the same slavery and persecution, putting even greater demands on God's people. Consequently, "the Israelites groaned in their slavery and cried out" (Exod. 2:23). What a pathetic picture! But this time, God responded. He "heard their groaning and he remembered his covenant with Abraham, with Isaac and with Jacob" (2:24). Now was the time God had planned to use Moses as a human instrument to carry out His divine plan.

A Time for Healing

Moses had lived a quiet and reclusive shepherd's life for forty years. What a contrast from his first four decades when he was at the center of Egyptian royalty—eating at the king's table, riding in the king's chariot, and commanding the king's army! During this second period in this rural setting, Moses probably forgot his painful experiences in Egypt. At least he didn't feel the intense emotional pain that always accompanies rejection. He had little reason to be afraid as he watched over a flock of sheep in the wilderness. His only threat came from wild animals, and Moses had not lost his physical strength. He could easily handle these challenges.

Moses certainly enjoyed his shepherd's life. Working with animals was quite different from working with people. In fact, he probably temporarily forgot how difficult people could be—how obstinate, how unpredictable, how fickle, and how cruel!

As I reflect on the emotional dynamics in Moses' life, I can't help but remember my own personal experiences as a young man. I grew up on a dairy farm before I entered Bible college. After graduating, I entered the ministry and encountered several Christian leaders—men I looked up to—who began to attack each another, not openly, but behind each other's backs. For one reason or another, each of these men confided in me. Being much younger and very inexperienced, I became horribly disillusioned. I took my eyes off of the Lord and even began to question what I believed.

During that crisis experience, I distinctly remember being tempted to leave the ministry, return to the farm, and work with animals. After all, I thought, they're at least "predictable." Dairy cows kick once in a while but usually for a good reason. I wasn't at all sure I wanted to continue working with people who, by contrast, seemed so unpredictable. Fortunately, the Lord had other plans, and in His own time He brought emotional healing into my life, restored my self-confidence, and opened some unusual doors for ministry. In retrospect, I now see that God was dealing with some weaknesses in my own life and at the same time preparing me for even greater challenges. This does not excuse the failure in the lives of these other men, but it illustrates how God can take mistakes, weaknesses, and sins in the lives of others—and in ourselves—and use these circumstances to achieve divine purposes.

Please don't misunderstand. With this illustration, I'm not at all comparing myself with Moses in terms of his spiritual stature and his great ministerial calling. However, I can identify with some of his emotional struggles. Most of us can. You see, God was dealing with Moses' human weaknesses and was also preparing him for a task—one that he could never carry out in his own strength.

The Burning Bush

When we are wounded emotionally, we can and do heal, especially when we have a place to regroup in an environment that is free from the factors that caused our pain in the first place. This also gives us an opportunity to learn to handle painful experiences more objectively. However, we're always vulnerable, especially when we're once again challenged to face the people who wounded us.

This certainly happened to Moses. Old emotional memories quickly surfaced the day God appeared to him in the burning bush and issued a call to be Israel's deliverer. This experience tore open old wounds. "Forgotten" fears once again gripped his heart.

Within moments, Moses began offering excuses. His reactions were defensive and resistant. The fact that he didn't want to respond indicates that he had probably concluded that when he was in Egypt, he had miscalculated God's will altogether. Not so! Though he was out of the will of God in terms of the way he went about it, he was within the will of God in being willing to be Israel's deliverer. Now was the time!

Resistance and Response (3:11–4:12)

Before we look at this dramatic dialogue between the God of the universe and a shepherd, let's get an overall perspective:

Resistance	Response
Moses: Who am I? (3:11)	God: I will be with you (3:12).
Moses: What shall I tell them? (3:13)	God: Say to the Israelites: "I AM has sent me to you" (3:14).
Moses: What if they do not believe me or listen to me? (4:1)	God: He gave Moses three signs: the rod that would become a serpent, the leprous hand that would become whole, and the water that would turn to blood (4:2–9).
Moses: I have never been eloquent . . . I am slow of speech and tongue (4:10).	God: I will help you speak and will teach you what to say (4:12).

Why did Moses resist God's call? Why did he make up these excuses? What was at the root of his problem? To get answers to these questions, let's look more closely.

The First Excuse

"Who am I?" What a contrast! Forty years earlier, Moses was so self-confident he had tried to deliver the children of Israel in his own strength. Now he felt so inferior and worthless that he believed that he was totally incapable of this great task.

Forty years before, Moses had looked at this job from the viewpoint of a very successful leader. If Josephus is correct, he had masterfully led the Egyptian army in victory over the Ethiopians. After all, he was the "son of Pharaoh's daughter"! He had been successful at everything. He believed he could deliver Israel from Egyptian bondage in his own strength.

But now, forty years later, Moses saw the task through the eyes of a shepherd. Life had been relatively easy for Moses in this new role. Sheep are certainly not known for rejecting the shepherd. And when wild animals attack (compared with human enemies), they are relatively easy to outsmart and drive away! This Moses had done many times.

The Root Problem

When Moses responded to the Lord with the question "Who am I?" he was reflecting more than a desire to escape from responsibility. Neither was it an act of humility. In actuality, Moses felt worthless and inferior, and lacked self-confidence. Down deep, he was still suffering from the rejection he had experienced so many years before.

Note that Moses wasn't remembering a traumatic experience from childhood. Rather, he was forty years old when he was rejected by the Egyptians and Israelites. His experience demonstrates that emotional pain can hit at any age and can affect us deeply no matter how secure our early years.

An Empathetic Ear

God understood Moses' struggle! This is the basic reason why He called to him from a burning bush. Though this was an unusual way to get Moses' attention, it was also a dramatic way to let Moses in on a very important truth: God can do anything!

The Lord responded to Moses empathetically but directly: "I will be with you," God said (3:12). You see, Moses still didn't understand why he had failed in his first mission. He had moved into action primarily because of his own successful experience, his training—and his self-confidence. He knew very little, if anything, of God's power and leadership in his life. He still needed to learn that lesson.

The Second Excuse

For most of us, a dramatic and direct word from God in the midst of a burning bush would be enough to get an enthusiastic response. But Moses' emotional and spiritual wounds were deep. Even though the Lord had assured him that He would enable him to succeed, he was not yet ready to respond positively. The Lord had just pulled the scab off of his "psychological strawberry." With predictable skepticism, he asked, *"What shall I say to them when they ask your name?"* (3:13, a paraphrase).

Though Moses was still resisting God's call, his reference to a "name" in his response indicates that he had learned at least one valuable lesson—one that would help him make proper decisions the rest of his life. Through his horrible failure forty years earlier, he knew that he at least needed an authority beyond himself. Though his "own name" had once been great in Egypt, and was still great even at that time, it did not carry enough clout to convince his own people that he was to be their deliverer. He needed a "Name" far more powerful than his own.

"I AM!"

God's answer to Moses' question was almost as dramatic as the burning bush: "God said to Moses, 'I AM WHO I AM. This is what you are to say to the Israelites: "I AM has sent me to you"'" (3:14).

God was telling Moses that He is the eternally existing one and always present to help His people. To a certain extent, God had already made this point with Moses when He had spoken earlier from the burning bush:

- "I am the God of your father, the God of Abraham, the God of Isaac and the God of Jacob." In other words, God was saying, "I AM the *covenantal* God of the *past!*" (3:6)
- "I have indeed seen the misery of my people in Egypt. I have heard them crying out because of their slave drivers, and I am concerned about their suffering." In other words, God was saying, "I AM the *compassionate* God of the *present!*" (3:7)
- "I have come down to rescue them from the hand of the Egyptians and to bring them up out of that land into a good and spacious land, a land flowing with milk and honey." In other words, God was saying, "I AM the *consummating* God of the *future!*" (3:8)

With these proclamations, God had illustrated His "I AM-ness" in words that Moses could grasp! God's eternal existence is difficult for any one of us to comprehend, but all of us can understand history. We all live "within history," which exists in space and time. This Moses could understand. But God wanted him to comprehend at least something about His eternality—that He existed before time began and that He would continue to exist when time is no more. Consequently, He gave this added explanation in response to Moses' question: "God also said to Moses, 'Say to the Israelites, "The LORD, the

God of your fathers—the God of Abraham, the God of Isaac and the God of Jacob—has sent me to you." This is my *name forever*, the name by which I am to be remembered from generation to generation'" (3:15).

The Third Excuse

At this point, Moses was convinced regarding God's power and His greatness. However, he was still not convinced he could persuade the children of Israel that God had sent him. Consequently, he asked another question: "What if they do not believe me or listen to me and say, 'The LORD did not appear to you'?" (4:1).

Moses' third excuse gives us a much clearer glimpse into his root problem. Forty years earlier, he had presented himself to the Israelites, assuming that they "would realize that God was using him to rescue them." However, "they did not" (Acts 7:25). Rather, they responded with a very sarcastic question: "Who made you ruler and judge over us?" (Exod. 2:14).

Moses still remembered those stinging words and the forceful hand that had "pushed" him "aside" (Acts 7:27). After forty years, feelings of fear that had long been suppressed suddenly surfaced and overwhelmed Moses.

In this dialogue, God demonstrated once again that He understood Moses' emotional pain and intense fear. In a sense, He would enable Moses to transport the "burning bush" to Egypt by enabling him to perform three dramatic and authenticating miracles in order to convince the children of Israel that he was on a divine mission. First, Moses would be able to turn the shepherd's staff into a serpent and again into a staff. Second, he would be able to cause his own hand to become leprous and then whole again. And third, he would be able to pour water on the ground taken from the sacred Nile and turn it into blood (Exod. 4:2–9). One sign could be interpreted as a trick, two as pure coincidence, but three? And each one so different? Moses quickly saw what God was doing, but he still had another concern—a major one!

The Fourth Excuse

Moses' final excuse reached to the depths of his troubled soul. His response is mixed with both denial and reality: "Moses said to the LORD, 'O Lord, I have never been eloquent, neither in the past nor since you have spoken to your servant. I am slow of speech and tongue'" (4:10).

Contrast Moses' response with Stephen's perspective on Moses' ability as a young man in Egypt. Rather than being "slow of speech and tongue," Moses "was powerful in speech and action" (Acts 7:22).

The picture is clear. As a leader in Egypt, Moses was very eloquent. He had been able to communicate fluently and to use words dramatically, but when he experienced such intense rejection, he had "lost his touch." He probably had forgotten how powerful he really was—certainly illustrating a form of denial. Otherwise, how could he dare to rationalize before the eternal God?

Why had Moses forgotten, at least temporarily? First, he had left the environment of Egypt over forty years before—an environment that was filled with educational opportunities and intellectual stimulation. He had constant exposure to the latest information and knowledge. He had regular dialogues with fellow Egyptians who were some of the greatest scholars in the world. But for forty years, Moses had been away from this environment. He had very little opportunity to practice the skills he had once used so capably. He had spent much of his time alone, shepherding a flock of sheep, which was not the most conducive atmosphere in which to maintain his verbal skills.

But there is another reason Moses actually "forgot" how fluent he really was. With rejection and loss of self-confidence come feelings of incompetence, which affect our ability to do what we once could do with fervor and excellence. Feelings of inferiority and insecurity have a dramatic effect on our ability to communicate effectively. Some believe that Moses actually had developed a stuttering problem—a belief which is certainly feasible. If he had, this only affirms the depth of his emotional pain.

Once again, God was sympathetic. However, the Lord's response indicates that He expected His servant to trust Him because of who He was. It's obvious Moses was testing the Lord's patience: "The LORD said to him, 'Who gave man his mouth? Who makes him deaf or mute? Who gives him sight or makes him blind? Is it not I, the LORD? *Now go*; I will help you *speak* and will *teach* you what to say'" (Exod. 4:11–12).

Reluctant Obedience

Moses was still not ready or willing to obey God. Though he submitted, he was reluctant. Furthermore, he wanted someone to go with him to speak for him and to assist him in doing what God wanted him to do alone (4:13).

At this moment, the Lord's impatience intensified and turned to anger (4:14). After all, He had miraculously appeared to him and spoke from a burning bush! He had patiently dialogued with Moses, answering every question— even promising him that He would enable him to work miracles once he arrived in Egypt, including the ability to speak clearly and forthrightly. But in spite of all these reassurances, Moses still hesitated to cooperate with God's will for his life.

But Moses was God's man for the job. The Lord told Moses his brother Aaron would assist him (4:14–5:1). Ultimately, as we will see in a future chapter, Moses' reluctance to do the job God had called him to do alone and the Lord's concession proved to be as much a burden for Moses as a blessing. Once the children of Israel left Egypt, Aaron got his brother—and the children of Israel—into serious trouble. In the end, God's *perfect will* is always better than His *permissive will.*

Becoming God's Man Today

Principles to Live By

This is perhaps one of the most practical sections in our study in the life of Moses. Though his specific experiences are far removed from any we'll ever encounter, we can all identify with his emotional reactions. God taught Moses powerful lessons when He appeared to him in a burning bush, and these lessons provide all of us with some very practical and encouraging principles.

Principle 1. God wants to use all of us in spite of our weaknesses.

Moses was a human being just like you and me. Even when his self-confidence was at zero and below, God used him. I'm glad for this lesson, aren't you? There is hope for *every* one of us. In spite of our shortcomings, our failures, our weaknesses, God can still use us.

Both the Bible and church history are filled with events and experiences that illustrate this principle. Joshua's whole body trembled when he was asked to lead the children of Israel into the promised land; yet he became one of God's greatest servants (Josh. 1:6–9). The apostle Paul was an insensitive, tough-minded Pharisee who stood watching while Stephen was stoned; yet he became the great apostle to the Gentiles (Acts 8:1). More recently, D. L. Moody had difficulty speaking "the king's English"; yet he became one of the greatest evangelists in history. Dr. M. R. DeHaan had a rough, gravelly voice; yet he became one of the greatest radio Bible teachers who has ever lived.

Obviously, we must be realistic regarding our handicaps. It would be foolish for a blind man to attempt to fly an airplane. It would be crazy for a 150-pound boxer to go into the ring with the heavyweight champion of the world. Yet, when it comes to doing God's work, let's remember the words of the apostle Paul, which seem diametrically opposed to the philosophy of leadership in the world: "For when I am weak, then I am strong" (2 Cor. 12:10b).

Principle 2. God wants all of us to balance self-confidence with God-confidence.

Moses went to two extremes. First, he said, "I can do it!" Then he said, "I can't do it!" For the Christian, both are true when stated properly. As Paul said, "I can do everything through him who gives me strength" (Phil. 4:13).

God wants us to believe in ourselves—our abilities and our talents. When young David went out to face Goliath, he knew he had great skill with a slingshot. He had practiced for hours out on a Judean hillside while watching his father's sheep. He could "split a hair" at a great distance. But when he approached the Philistine giant, he also knew he needed God's supernatural strength to win this battle. This is why he told King Saul, "The LORD who delivered me from the paw of the lion and the paw of the bear will deliver me from the hand of this Philistine" (1 Sam. 17:37). And this is why David cried out with great confidence as he approached Goliath: "You come against me with sword and spear and javelin, but I come against you in the name of the LORD Almighty, the God of the armies of Israel, whom you have defied. *This day the LORD will hand you over to me*" (17:45–46a).

When Nehemiah began to rebuild the wall of Jerusalem, he faced what appeared to be an impossible task. Morale was low. The enemies of Israel were consistently threatening an attack. But Nehemiah worked hard to lay out an ingenious plan. He led the wall builders to work day and night, laying bricks with one hand and holding a spear in the other. However, through the entire process, Nehemiah repeatedly reminded the people that they could complete this task with God's help. The Lord would protect them and give them strength. And what is even more amazing, after they had completed the task in an incredible fifty-two days, their "enemies . . . lost *their* self-confidence, because they realized that this work had been done with the help of our God" (Neh. 6:16).

In some respects, maintaining balance between self-confidence and God-confidence is like riding a bicycle on a tightwire, but it's exciting—and possible. It's also a divine mystery and a unique experience for every Christian. This is why Paul wrote: "I have been crucified with Christ and I no longer live, but Christ lives in me. The life I live in the body, I live by faith in the Son of God, who loved me and gave himself for me" (Gal. 2:20).

Principle 3. God wants us to be able to overcome the negative results of rejection and become men He can use to achieve His purposes in this world.

Moses was a very sensitive man by nature. And sensitive people are affected the most by negative experiences. Even as a grown man who had a secure background, Moses was wounded deeply when he was rejected in Egypt. Though buried deep within, he carried this pain with him and developed a personality weakness that interfered with God's plan for his life. Furthermore, he began to use his problem as an excuse to avoid doing God's will.

All of us can identify with Moses' problem. All of us have weaknesses in our personalities that cause us to draw back, to refuse to act responsibly, and to fail to do what we know we should do. Our tendency is to rationalize our behavior, just like Moses did, and even fail to take advantage of the opportunities God gives us to overcome our problems.

Timothy was this kind of young man. He was definitely sensitive by nature. And when he saw Paul stoned in his hometown in Lystra, it certainly impacted his life (Acts 14:19–20).

He was often fearful, even as a dedicated missionary. This is why Paul often encouraged him to be strong and brave. Even in Paul's final letter to Timothy—just before this great apostle faced martyrdom—he penned these words to Timothy: "For God did not give us a spirit of timidity, but a spirit of power, of love and of self-discipline. So do not be ashamed to testify about our Lord, or ashamed of me his prisoner" (2 Tim. 1:7–8).

Principle 4. God wants to use our failures to prepare us to face greater challenges.

Moses failed to see what God was attempting to accomplish in his life. The Lord was taking a bad experience, one of Moses' own making, and was using it to equip him for his future ministry. God knew that Moses' rejection in Egypt forty years before would fade into "nothingness" in view of the rejection he would face in the future as he began carrying out God's will in leading the children of Israel out of Egypt and through the wilderness. The fear that caused Moses to resist God's will, as well as the experience of God's power to overcome that fear, would become a strength that the Lord would use in his life to enable him to handle even greater problems in the future.

God knows our weaknesses, and I'm convinced that He often allows us to experience pain and difficulties in these areas in order to face greater challenges more victoriously. Though we may always be vulnerable in these areas, we can learn to handle crises more effectively and to rebound more quickly! In other words, trials enable us to get ready to take another step upward in carrying out God's divine plan.

Personalizing These Principles

As you reflect on Moses' problems outlined in this chapter, with which one do you identify most? Ask the Holy Spirit to speak clearly to your heart as you complete this exercise:

❑ 1. Moses' inability to see how God could use him—with all of his weaknesses and failures.

❑ 2. Moses' problem of balancing "self-confidence" with "God (Christ)-confidence."

❑ 3. Moses' inferiority complex.

❑ 4. Moses' inability to see how God was using past failures to equip him for future service.

Set a Goal

Now that you've completed this exercise, what one goal do you need to set for your life?

_____

_____

_____

_____

Memorize the Following Scripture

I have been crucified with Christ and I no longer live, but Christ lives in me. The life I live in the body, I live by faith in the Son of God, who loved me and gave himself for me.
GAL. 2:20

Growing Together

1. How has rejection impacted your ability to respond to the challenges that God is bringing into your life?

2. What kind of experience precipitated this rejection? What caused it? Who was at fault?

3. How have you handled this rejection?

4. What divine purpose can you see in this negative experience—even though you had nothing to do with it?

5. How can we pray for you specifically?

Chapter 5

The Importance of a
Good Self-Image
Read Exodus 4:27–14:31

God wants us to feel good about ourselves! He knows full well that unless we move forward trusting in the abilities and strength God has given us, we'll often fail to tackle the tough tasks that face us in life—and serving God is often a tough task! There are times we must turn our faces into the blistering wind—even a blustering storm—and march straight forward. In fact, Jesus said: "If anyone would come after me, he must deny himself *and take up his cross daily* and follow me" (Luke 9:23).

Unless we have "self-confidence," we'll even have difficulty picking up our cross on a regular basis. But for Christians, this "confidence" is not the same "confidence" that is the theme of so many motivational addresses. It's a "confidence" that is rooted in a secure relationship with God through Jesus Christ. Paul illustrated this kind of confidence in his own life when he wrote: "I can do everything through him who gives me strength" (Phil. 4:13).

Before God could use him, Moses had to learn this lesson. When he tried to deliver the children of Israel from Egypt the first time, he did not have a secure relationship with his heavenly Father. In fact, he was just coming to know the God of Abraham, Isaac, and Jacob. Though he had heard about the one true God from his parents, he had not experienced what it really means to trust God and to walk with Him—like Enoch and Noah (Gen. 5:21; 6:9). He had learned to trust in himself. His security was in his own abilities. Consequently, for the first time in his life, he experienced utter failure. As a result, he suffered emotionally because of the intense rejection from his own people as well as the Egyptians. He lost his self-confidence.

Forty years in the wilderness as a shepherd certainly brought a measure of healing. Moses was free from the burdens and pressures that always accompany a high profile leadership position. But this experience was only laying the foundation for God to rebuild his self-image.

Moses was definitely a "marked" man! God had plans for him—plans that would call for unusual self-confidence rooted in his confidence and faith in God. But clearly, Moses was not yet ready for this task emotionally or spiritually. When God called to him from the burning bush, he responded with excuses. But God understood. He patiently, but directly, began to help Moses develop a divine outlook on the great task—the *tough task*—he had ahead of him, the awesome responsibility of leading the children of Israel out of Egypt, through the wilderness, and into the promised land.

Moses finally acquiesced to God's call—not because of a restored self-image and self-confidence—but because of God's gentle but persistent demands and promises. In fact, God finally consented to allow Moses' brother, Aaron, assist him in communicating with both the children of Israel and with Pharaoh.

Getting His Household in Order

Before Moses left for Egypt, he shared what was happening with his father-in-law. He sought Jethro's permission to take his wife and two sons back to Egypt. Maintaining his relationship with his father-in-law was very important to Moses and, as we'll see, it paid dividends in the future in ways neither anticipated. Though Jethro certainly faced the normal ambivalence that accompanies this kind of separation, he responded positively. "Go," he said, "and I wish you well" (Exod. 4:18–19).

While Moses and his little family were "on the way," and before he met Aaron in the desert, Moses faced an unusual test. God had made it clear to Moses that he should circumcise both of his sons. He evidently had performed this rite on his older son, but when he was about to circumcise his youngest, his wife, Zipporah, resisted. Coming out of a pagan background, she believed this rite that had been established by God with Abraham as a sign of the covenant was a bloody and unnecessary ritual (Gen. 17:9–14). She was obviously disgusted and angry. Moses evidently succumbed to her resistance rather than obeying God.

The Lord was extremely displeased with Moses. The historical record is very direct in that we're told that "the LORD met Moses and was about to kill him" (4:24). More than likely, the Lord allowed Moses to be struck with a death-threatening disease—which definitely got Zipporah's attention. Seeing that her husband was about to die, she angrily grabbed "a flint knife" and circumcised her son and then threw the foreskin at Moses' feet. At that moment, God spared Moses' life! (4:26).

The lesson is clear. Before Moses was ready to face the children of Israel and an evil man like Pharaoh, he had to get his own household in order. He had to become the spiritual leader. He couldn't allow his wife's rejection of him and the Lord to dominate and control his behavior—especially when it caused him to make decisions that were contrary to the will of God. After all, circumcision was the sign of God's covenant with Abraham and all Israel. How could Moses deliver the children of Israel from Egypt if he were not willing to follow God's will at this fundamental and foundational point of obedience?

Preliminary Tests

Before Moses was ready to announce the ten plagues to Pharaoh and become the channel through whom God would unleash His mighty power and fury upon an unbelieving and pagan people, he needed some initial tests that would strike directly at the heart of his problem—his inferiority complex that had been brought on by rejection. Notice how precisely the following events—or tests—zero in on Moses' weakness (Exod. 4:27–7:14).

The First Test—Painful Memories

As soon as Moses returned to Egypt with Aaron, they did what God had commanded (4:27–28). They "brought together all the elders of the Israelites, and Aaron told them everything the LORD had said to Moses. He also performed the signs before the people" (4:29–30). Aaron not only became a spokesman for Moses, but God transferred His power to Aaron who was able to perform the three miraculous signs He had promised Moses (Exod. 4:1–9).

What happened next was very reassuring. The children of Israel "believed" what Aaron had to say. In fact, "they bowed down and worshiped" (4:31). What a welcome contrast this must have been for Moses in comparison with the rejection he had experienced forty years earlier! He must have breathed a sigh of relief.

But this first test had two parts. Confronting Pharaoh was another story. The king rejected God's message through Moses and Aaron. He even put a greater burden on the children of Israel, insisting that they produce the same number of bricks without having the necessary materials. They had to maintain the same quota in production, but they had to gather the materials to make the bricks (Exod. 5:1–18).

Predictably, the children of Israel reacted with anger. They turned against Moses and Aaron, spewing out strong and bitter words: "'May the LORD look upon you and judge you!'" they cried out! "'You have made us a stench to Pharaoh and his officials and have put a sword in their hand to kill us'" (5:21).

Imagine what must have happened to Moses. Their reactions certainly surfaced bitter and frightening memories. A strong urge must have flooded his entire being—an urge to hide, to run, to once again escape to a foreign land and become a quiet and gentle shepherd, free from the pressure and tension of this awesome leadership responsibility.

Moses *did* run! But this time, he ran in the right direction—straight to his source of strength. "'Oh, Lord,'" he cried, "'Why have you brought trouble upon this people? Is this why you sent me? Ever since I went to Pharaoh to speak in your name, he has brought trouble upon this people, and you have not rescued your people at all'" (5:22–23).

Understandably, Moses was disillusioned and confused. He also lacked faith—and his memory failed—two dynamics that often go together. He forgot what God had told him from the burning bush—that upon his initial encounter with Pharaoh, the king would not allow the children of Israel to leave Egypt (Exod. 3:19–20). In other words, Moses should not have been surprised at Pharaoh's reaction. But now all Moses could remember was the rejection and the subsequent pain and the anxiety he had felt before.

But Moses was making progress. Rather than trying to escape, like Jonah who headed for Nineveh, he turned to the Lord for answers. He poured out his anxiety to the only one who could answer his questions (5:22–23).

God understood Moses' feelings—and He was pleased with his response. There is no evidence that He became angry with Moses' honesty. He simply moved him on to face the next challenge in leading His people from Egyptian bondage; but unknown to Moses, it would be another personal test.

The Second Test—More Rejection

After this first painful experience, the Lord reiterated His plan to Moses. He *would* deliver the children of Israel from Egyptian bondage (Exod. 6:1–5). But with this reassuring word came another painful directive. God spelled out Moses' next assignment: "'Therefore, say to the Israelites: "I am the LORD, and I will bring you out from under the yoke of the Egyptians. I will free you from being slaves to them, and I will redeem you with an outstretched arm and with mighty acts of judgment. . . . And I will bring you to the land I swore with uplifted hand to give to Abraham, to Isaac and to Jacob. I will give it to you as a possession. I am the LORD"'" (6:6, 8).

Moses obeyed God and delivered this message to the children of Israel, certainly with a great deal of fear, anxiety, and ambivalence. But imagine how he felt when this time the children of Israel rejected his message. We read that "they did not listen" to Moses "because of their discouragement and cruel bondage" (6:9).

While Moses was reeling from this rejection, the Lord gave him another directive, which must have seemed like the final blow: "'Go, tell Pharaoh king of Egypt to let the Israelites go out of his country'" (6:10).

God's command was so painful that Moses regressed to his final excuse that he offered God that day when He had spoken to him from the burning bush:

"'If the Israelites will not listen to me, why would Pharaoh listen to me, *since I speak with faltering lips?*'" (4:10; 6:12, 30).

The Third Test—Moving in the Right Direction

God's response to Moses' regression was very similar to the way He handled his excuses when they dialogued together at the burning bush. There's no evidence that God condemned Moses. He kept reassuring him and encouraging him to continue to do His will (Exod. 7:1–13).

God responded by telling Moses it was time to impress Pharaoh. The king needed a dose of God's power. Moses was to take his staff and throw it down before Pharaoh, and it would "become a snake" (7:9). At this point, Moses did not hesitate. He obeyed immediately. But more importantly, Moses quickly rebounded from his feelings of rejection. He was making progress in developing both confidence in himself, and most importantly, in the God he was learning to trust and serve.

God had already predicted what Pharaoh would do. He rejected the miracle. But now Moses was ready to move on to the main events—to be the instrument God would use to cause Pharaoh to let His people go—a process that would ironically put the finishing touches on Moses' emotional and spiritual rehabilitation.

God's Divine Therapy

God allowed Moses and Aaron to bring ten supernatural and awesome plagues on Egypt (Exod. 7:14–12:37). God's primary purpose is clear. He was convincing Israel, the Egyptians—and the whole world—that He was the one true God (Exod. 9:16; Rom. 9:17)! But, as we've already noted regarding the preliminary tests, God was also carrying out a secondary purpose within this divine process. He was rebuilding Moses' self-image!

It's easy to miss seeing how all of this happened in Moses' life. The miracles and plagues that God brought on the Egyptians are so overwhelming that they overshadow the way in which God was working in Moses' life. But as you'll see, God was not only demonstrating His great power to Israel and to the Egyptians, but He was at work in the life of a man He loved, restoring his self-confidence and preparing him for one of the greatest tasks ever faced by any human being.

As you read the following biblical statements, you can see beyond the fireworks! Though Aaron began the process,

Moses quickly emerged as the primary spokesman as well as the one God used to work the miracles. By the end of the third plague, God was already speaking directly to Pharaoh through Moses, and Moses, rather than Aaron, was directly involved in performing the miracles. In the process of bringing these plagues on Egypt, God brought His servant Moses to the place where he was carrying out the task He had originally called him to do—and almost totally without Aaron's assistance. It's a remarkable lesson in "divine therapy."

Following are the statements under each plague that clearly show this evolving pattern (emphasis added):

The Ten Plagues

1. The Plague of Water to Blood

7:14 "Then the LORD said to *Moses*"

7:19 "The LORD said to *Moses*, 'Tell Aaron, "Take your staff and stretch out your hand over the waters of Egypt"'"

2. The Plague of Frogs

8:5 "Then the LORD said to *Moses*, 'Tell Aaron, "Stretch out your hand"'"

8:6 "*So Aaron stretched out his hand*"

3. The Plague of Gnats

8:16 "Then the LORD said to *Moses*, 'Tell Aaron, "Stretch out your staff"'"

8:17 "Aaron stretched out his hand with the staff"
[Note: From this point forward, Moses spoke directly to Pharaoh without Aaron's assistance.]

4. The Plague of Insects

8:20 "Then the LORD said to *Moses*"

8:26 "But *Moses* said"

8:29 "*Moses* answered"

8:30 "*Then Moses left Pharaoh and prayed to the LORD*"

5. The Plague of Pestilence

9:1   "Then the LORD said to *Moses*"

6. The Plague of Boils

9:8   "Then the LORD said to *Moses* and Aaron, 'Take handfuls of soot from a furnace and have Moses toss it into the air in the presence of Pharaoh'"

9:10   "*Moses tossed it into the air*"

[Note: This is the first miracle where Moses both spoke and participated with a physical gesture. Up to this point, Aaron had stretched out his hand or staff. Notice also that Aaron helped him get started and then let Moses toss the soot into the air.]

7. The Plague of Hail

9:13   "Then the LORD said to *Moses*"
9:22   "Then the LORD said to *Moses*"
9:23   "*Moses stretched out his staff*"

8. The Plague of Locusts

10:1   "Then the LORD said to *Moses*"
10:3   "So *Moses* and Aaron . . . said"
10:12 "And the LORD said to *Moses*"
10:13 "*So Moses stretched out his staff over Egypt*"

9. The Plague of Darkness

10:21 "Then the LORD said to *Moses*"
10:22 "*So Moses stretched out his hand toward the sky*"

10. The Plague of Death

11:1   "Now the LORD had said to *Moses*"
11:4   "*So Moses said, 'This is what the Lord says'*"

Blending Self-Confidence with God-Confidence

Following this incredible experience, Moses definitely had a greater degree of self-esteem. Note first that his ability to respect himself directly correlated with the way in which he was respected and accepted in Egypt. In fact, by the end of the ninth plague, we read that "Moses himself was highly regarded in Egypt by Pharaoh's officials and by the people" (11:3).

Closely aligned with all of this was Moses' ability to trust and obey God and to feel comfortable carrying out God's will. Little by little God rebuilt Moses' self-image until he was able to speak clearly and forcefully and to step out by faith and perform miracles. Furthermore, he was able to handle murmuring and criticism—not without pain, but without allowing rejection to interfere with his ability to carry out God's will.

The Big Test

The greatest evidence of how far Moses had come emotionally and spiritually is very clear when the Egyptians pursued the children of Israel as they were leaving Egypt. The Red Sea was in front of them, and the Egyptian army was coming up fast behind them. From a human point of view, there was absolutely no way to escape (14:1–10).

Terror overtook the Israelites—then, anger! But against whom? Predictably, it was against Moses. But, this was one of the great moments God had been preparing Moses to face victoriously! A year earlier he might have crumbled under the pressure. But not now! This was one test he wouldn't fail.

Listen to the complaints from the children of Israel and try to walk in Moses' sandals. How would you have felt? "As Pharaoh approached, the Israelites looked up, and there were the Egyptians, marching after them. They were terrified and cried out to the LORD. They said to Moses, 'Was it because there were no graves in Egypt that you brought us to the desert to die? What have you done to us by bringing us out of

Egypt? Didn't we say to you in Egypt, "Leave us alone; let us serve the Egyptians"? It would have been better for us to serve the Egyptians than to die in the desert!'" (14:10–12).

And now listen to Moses' instant response, reflecting both self-confidence and most of all, trust in Jehovah: "Moses answered the people, 'Do not be afraid. Stand firm and you will see the deliverance the LORD will bring you today. The Egyptians you see today you will never see again. The LORD will fight for you; you need only to be still'" (14:13–14).

At this point, Moses stretched out his staff—that marvelous symbol of God's power—and the sea divided. The children of Israel marched across on dry ground. And once on the other side, Moses stretched out his staff again and caused the powerful waters to rush in on the Egyptians, drowning both horses and riders (14:15–28).

Israel was safe. At last, they were free from Egyptian bondage (14:29–30). And when they "saw the great power the LORD displayed against the Egyptians, the people feared the LORD and put their trust in him and in Moses his servant" (14:31).

What a great victory for Moses both spiritually and emotionally! The people once again trusted Moses—and trust is something every leader needs in order to feel comfortable and to lead effectively. More importantly, they transferred their trust in Moses to God.

Becoming God's Man Today

Principles to Live By

This dramatic section of Scripture yields a number of principles that we can apply to our lives today. Though we'll never face the incredible challenges Moses faced, we'll confront situations that create similar feelings. In this sense, emotional and spiritual problems are relative. A much less significant event in our lives can lead to the same immobilizing fear that interfered with Moses' ability to respond to God's will.

*Principle 1. God is concerned that emotional problems
such as insecurity, inferiority feelings, and anxiety
do not stand in our way of trusting and obeying Him.*

The Lord is interested in every problem we face. He wants us to carry out His will, trusting Him to enable us to be victorious over the forces of evil. He does not want our emotional problems to hold us back spiritually.

*Principle 2. Emotional healing is normally a process
that takes time.*

Today, some Christians believe that conversion to Christ automatically solves all psychological problems. This is simply not true. As we've seen, it took time for God to bring healing into Moses' life. And even when the Lord was performing unbelievable miracles in Egypt, He still used a natural process to restore Moses' public image, his self-confidence, and a proper perspective on God Himself.

*Principle 3. During the process of overcoming emotional
problems, it sometimes gets worse before it gets better.*

This was also true of Moses. It was painful to face God's call and to fail some of the initial tests. But it was necessary to "fail" smaller tests so he could pass the big one. If he had failed at the Red Sea, humanly speaking, there would have been no way to recover.

*Principle 4. It is easy to regress to earlier patterns
of behavior when we face the circumstances
that caused the problem in the first place.*

As we've seen, Moses regressed. And so will we. But if we're making steady progress, our ability to rebound will become easier and quicker.

*Principle 5. Being accepted by others is basic to developing
our self-acceptance and self-confidence.*

Again, we see this sequence in the way God dealt with Moses. The first thing the Lord did was to enable Moses to convince the children of Israel he was their deliverer. Though he used Aaron to build this bridge, "being accepted" by the children of Israel was an important first step in being able to "feel good" about the incredible task that lay before him. How could he lead people who didn't believe in him? And how could he believe in himself without knowing his followers believed in him? More importantly, how could he move forward with confidence unless the children of Israel believed God had sent him to be their deliverer?

Principle 6. Self-confidence and self-acceptance are basic to being able to feel comfortable trusting and obeying God.

This sequence in itself may make us "feel uncomfortable." After all, shouldn't how we feel about ourselves be based on how we feel about our relationship with God? But the facts are, Moses' ability to trust God was based—not on the burning bush per se—but on how he felt about his own abilities. This is why God used Aaron to help Moses in the initial steps. God did not bypass the human process He has designed to enable us to feel comfortable trusting Him.

This brings into focus the importance of the intimate relationships that should be fostered in a Christian family. God uses fathers particularly to meet our emotional and social needs. Feeling comfortable and being able to trust our natural fathers is foundational in enabling us to feel comfortable and to trust our Heavenly Father—the Father we cannot see.

This is God's ideal plan. However, this is why God has also developed plan B—the family of God. People who do not have secure family relationships can experience acceptance and love and emotional healing within the body of Jesus Christ. In turn, these secure relationships with Christians enables believers to feel comfortable with God. True and vital

Christianity is relational, and relational Christianity is necessary to produce mature Christian personalities who learn to love and trust God.

Principle 7. God understands emotional problems and He is very patient with His children.

Clearly this was true in Moses' life. God gently led him step by step as He rebuilt Moses' self-image. On the other hand, God will not tolerate consistent irresponsible behavior, especially when He provides us with opportunities to overcome our problems. We're asking for trouble if we constantly ignore God's help. Probably the most serious result will be that eventually God will simply allow us to go on in our self-pity and insecurity.

Principle 8. When attempting to overcome problems of insecurity, we may need a temporary "crutch" to help us develop our own self-confidence as well as our trust in God.

Moses needed an "Aaron," and God provided him with one. But remember, God's preference was that Moses depend primarily on Him—not on Aaron. This is why God enabled Moses to take on more and more responsibility in their confrontations with Pharaoh.

Principle 9. When supporting and helping others with problems of insecurity, we must withdraw our support gradually and sensitively.

Again, we see how God did this with Moses. In the beginning phases, Aaron took the primary responsibility. However, little by little, Aaron moved out of a lead position and stood by Moses' side. Eventually, Moses was out front and Aaron was his assistant.

Principle 10. No matter what our maturity level, we are always vulnerable, particularly in the areas where we once were weak.

In Moses' early life, his greatest strength was security, which led him to make a serious mistake. Because of his traumatic experience, his greatest weakness became insecurity, which continued to be his area of vulnerability. As we continue to follow the story of Moses, we'll see how this happened.

Principle 11. We are never too old to allow God to begin to develop our self-confidence and to rebuild our self-image.

We must remember that Moses was eighty years old when God began this process in his life. How old are you?

Personalizing These Principles

Reread the eleven principles that flow from Moses' experience. As you do, ask the Holy Spirit to make clear which ones are most relevant in your own life and place a check mark by those that seem most applicable.

Set a Goal

As you reflect on the principles you've checked, what one goal do you need to set for your life?

_____

_____

_____

_____

Memorize the Following Scripture

Brothers, I do not consider myself yet to have taken hold of it. But one thing I do: Forgetting what is behind and straining

*toward what is ahead, I press on toward the goal to win the
prize for which God has called me heavenward in Christ Jesus.*
PHILIPPIANS 3:13–14

Growing Together

1. How has God helped you overcome bouts with insecurity and feelings of inferiority?

2. Do you have any areas in your emotional life where you are particularly vulnerable? Would you feel free to share what they are and why these are areas of vulnerability?

3. How can we maintain a proper balance between having self-confidence and at the same time having a strong faith in God? How can we recognize imbalance?

4. What can we do for each other to help all of us maintain this balance?

5. How can we pray for you specifically?

Chapter 6

A True Test of Maturity
Read Exodus 15:1–21

*H*ave you noticed how some people consistently talk about themselves and their own achievements? In fact, they have difficulty honoring others and very seldom, if ever, give God the glory for the blessings in their lives.

There seem to be at least two reasons for this tendency. On the one hand, people like this are just plain arrogant and self-centered! They have been the center of attention so long, they have difficulty sharing the limelight with anyone else— including God.

On the other hand, some of these people are very insecure. Underneath, they really feel like a failure. Their self-image is at a low ebb. To hear them talk, you'd never guess this is their problem. In actuality, their self-absorption is their effort at building themselves up in their own eyes and in the eyes of others. They're trying to feel good about who they are.

In both situations, these people focus on themselves— which often brings rejection. People tend to ignore people like this. Sadly, those who have a self-image problem to begin with end up in a vicious spiral downward. Rather than gaining respect—which they so desperately want and need—they lose it even more.

People who are starved for attention and who have a poor self-image have another temptation—to take credit for things they didn't do. Moses faced this moment in his own life. It certainly happened after he had led the children of Israel out of Egypt and to victory on the other side of the Red Sea.

Think for a moment what had happened since God appeared to him in a burning bush on the backside of the desert. Moses had resisted the Lord's call! "I can't do it!" he cried. "I'm not capable!" But now, with the Red Sea before him and the Egyptian army coming up behind, Moses cried out to the children of Israel, "'Do not be afraid. Stand firm and you will see the deliverance the LORD will bring you today'" (Exod. 14:13).

Moses had come a long, long way from being so insecure he couldn't speak properly to being a man whose self-image had been restored. He had taken giant steps toward being both psychologically and spiritually mature. The true test of his maturity is seen in how he handled success. He honored God for *all* of his achievements. Moses' song—which he wrote following their great victory over the Egyptians—clearly illustrates this truth.

A Song of Victory (15:1–21)

Moses' education in Egypt certainly included the arts, which is demonstrated in his ability to compose both beautiful poetry and meaningful music when he wrote a song after they had crossed over the Red Sea. It has a single theme, which is focused in the chorus. It is stated twice—once at the beginning of the song and once at the end when Miriam led all of the women in singing and dancing. It's a beautiful reprise: "'I will sing to the Lord, for he is highly exalted. The horse and its rider he has hurled into the sea'" (15:1, 21).

The meaning in this theme is very clear. The Lord had been greatly exalted and honored through this significant event. Consequently, the children of Israel used this song for praise and adoration. The event, of course, was the Egyptian defeat—and it is succinctly summarized in the second line: "The horse and its rider he has hurled into the sea."

We're not told specifically how the children of Israel presented and performed this song. However, it's feasible that after each stanza, the women of Israel, led by Moses' sister Miriam, broke forth with dancing and singing, repeating the theme chorus that Moses recorded at the beginning and the end (15:20–21).

Moses developed this theme with three stanzas. Each stanza, in turn, has a sub-theme. Each sub-theme is followed by a detailed description of how God had won this great victory over Egypt, hurling the "horse and its rider . . . into the sea."

The First Stanza

The Sub-theme: (15:2)

> *The LORD is my strength and my song;*
> *he has become my salvation.*
> *He is my God, and I will praise him,*
> *my father's God, and I will exalt him.*

The Sub-theme Paraphrased:
They were delivered by God's strength and power.

The Detailed Description: (15:3–5)

> *The LORD is a warrior;*
> *the LORD is his name.*
> *Pharaoh's chariots and his army*
> *he has hurled into the sea;*
> *The best of Pharaoh's officers*
> *are drowned in the Red Sea.*
> *The deep waters have covered them;*
> *they sank to the depths like a stone.*

The Second Stanza

The Sub-theme: (15:6)

> *Your right hand, O LORD,*
> *   was majestic in power.*
> *Your right hand, O LORD,*
> *   shattered the enemy.*

The Sub-theme Paraphrased:

God's righteous anger is eventually unleashed against those who continually resist Him and fight against Him.

The Detailed Description: (15:7–10)

> *In the greatness of your majesty*
> *   you threw down those who opposed you.*
> *You unleashed your burning anger;*
> *   it consumed them like stubble.*
> *By the blast of your nostrils*
> *   the waters piled up.*
> *The surging waters stood firm like a wall;*
> *   the deep waters congealed in the heart of the sea.*
> *The enemy boasted,*
> *   "I will pursue, I will overtake them.*
> *I will divide the spoils;*
> *   I will gorge myself on them.*
> *I will draw my sword*
> *   and my hand will destroy them."*
> *But you blew with your breath,*
> *   and the sea covered them.*
> *They sank like lead*
> *   in the mighty waters.*

The Third Stanza

The Sub-theme: (15:11)

> *Who among the gods is like you, O LORD?*
> *Who is like you—*
> *majestic in holiness,*
> *awesome in glory,*
> *working wonders?*

The Sub-theme Paraphrased:

God is the one true and eternal God, the only one who is holy, to be feared, and who is able to work great miracles.

The Detailed Description: (15:12–18)

> *You stretched out your right hand*
> *and the earth swallowed them.*
> *In your unfailing love you will lead*
> *the people you have redeemed.*
> *In your strength you will guide them*
> *to your holy dwelling.*
> *The nations will hear and tremble;*
> *anguish will grip the people of Philistia.*
> *The chiefs of Edom will be terrified,*
> *the leaders of Moab will be seized with trembling,*
> *the people of Canaan will melt away;*
> *terror and dread will fall upon them.*
> *By the power of your arm*
> *they will be as still as a stone—*
> *until your people pass by, O LORD,*
> *until the people you bought pass by.*
> *You will bring them in and plant them*
> *on the mountain of your inheritance—*
> *the place, O LORD, you made for your dwelling,*
> *the sanctuary, O Lord, your hands established.*
> *The LORD will reign*
> *for ever and ever.*

Reflections of Maturity

In the previous chapter, we've already noted how easy it is to miss the way in which God rebuilt Moses' self-image—simply because of the awesome and sensational nature of the ten plagues. Just so, we can easily miss one of the greatest lessons in this song of victory—a reflection of Moses' spiritual and psychological maturity.

Let's review what has happened. Moses moved from a position of fear and almost total dependence on his brother Aaron to the place where he alone became God's spokesman and human instrument in performing miracles. It was Moses, the once timid shepherd, who with fantastic confidence and faith in God stretched out his staff over the Red Sea. Once on the other side, it was Moses who again stretched out his staff and the waters came rushing in on the Egyptian army. It was this same Moses who sat down with heartfelt adoration and praise to God and penned this song of victory. And when he did, Moses let us in on what had happened to him personally. In this song we see some outstanding reflections of his spiritual and psychological maturity.

His Relationship with God

Was it not Moses, the man, who had stretched out his hand and precipitated the plague of insects? Had he not thrown the soot into the sky, bringing the plague of boils? Wasn't it Moses who stretched out his staff and the lightning began to flash, the thunder roared, and the hail began to fall? And in that final great plague, it was Moses who announced the plague of death that smote all the firstborn Egyptians. Finally in this dramatic scenario, it was Moses who stretched out his hand over the Red Sea, dividing that great span of water into a huge chasm!

But where is Moses' name in the song of victory? Obviously, it does not appear—and for a good reason. Moses had learned that he—or any man—is just an instrument in

God's hands, an instrument that can only function with God's permission and assistance. Consequently, Moses' song is *to the Lord* and *about the Lord*—and about what *He had done* for Israel. In the New International Version of the Bible, the name of the Lord God of Israel appears thirteen times in this song. In addition, there are thirty-three pronouns (Him, He, His, You, Your)—a total of forty-six references to the Lord Himself!

This song then reflects Moses' mature perspective regarding himself and his relationship to God. Some forty years before, he had tried to deliver Israel with his own "right hand," striking down an Egyptian taskmaster. He had set out to be the deliverer in his own strength. And now forty years later, Moses set the record straight when he said: "'*Your right hand, O LORD*, was majestic in power. *Your right hand, O LORD*, shattered the enemy'" (15:6).

Don't misunderstand: God used Moses' mouth, his abilities, his personality—and even his "right arm." But Moses knew who really made it all possible. This is true humility!

His Relationship with the Children of Israel

Moses' maturity was not only theological but very practical. He did not make statements in the song about God as the deliverer that were simply pious phrases. They were words of action. These words were reflective of his lifestyle—not just his verbalizations.

Moses could now handle success as well as failure. This is a true mark of maturity. If Moses had succeeded too soon as the great leader of Israel, particularly in his early years of life, he may have been carried away with pride and self-glorification, which would have been his downfall! But God had been preparing him for this moment of glory and prestige—a moment he could handle with true humility. He had learned his lesson well. Forty years before, his attitudes of superiority had been shattered. But God slowly and steadily rebuilt his self-image and brought him to the place of true perspective regarding both his relationship with God and with man.

Moses' maturity is also evident in his awareness that Israel would be tempted to glorify him—to perhaps even make him their god-king. The scriptural record makes it very clear that following the Red Sea adventure, the people not only "feared the LORD," but they "put their trust in him and in *Moses his servant*" (14:31). Remember also that most of the people in Israel were still very carnal. After years of exposure to pagan gods and a licentious, worldly lifestyle, they were far from ready to respond maturely to so great a deliverance.

Consider this moment of opportunism for Moses! From a worldly point of view, this was his opportunity to become a great man in the eyes of men—not only among the children of Israel, but among the pagan nations as well. After all, Moses was the one who had spoken, who had held out his hand, and who had held out his staff for all to hear and see. No one who was observing this incredible drama could miss seeing the connection between Moses "the leader" and what happened in Egypt and to the Red Sea.

Moses guarded against this misinterpretation by writing a song that reflected the truth. If Israel took the words of this song seriously—and I believe they did—there would be no way for them to focus their eyes on Moses rather than God. They, of course, knew that Moses was involved, and they believed in him. But now they saw Moses in proper perspective. He was serving the eternal God!

Becoming God's Man Today

Principles to Live By

Moses' song teaches all of us three important lessons. All three principles relate to how we view ourselves in relationship to God and others. In essence, when we have a proper self-image that is centered in God, we have nothing to prove! God's glory and the accomplishments of others are far more important than our own.

Principle 1. As men, we'll always face the challenge of maintaining a proper view of ourselves in relationship to God.

Ask the average man what he has accomplished, and he'll tell you. Pick up the average history or science book and you'll discover what we think of ourselves. Look for the name of God, and you may look in vain—particularly as we have revised history. Generally speaking, we do not acknowledge God's role in our accomplishments. Rather, we acknowledge ourselves.

It's true that we've accomplished great things in this century. We've discovered nuclear power and how to harness that power. We've made great advances in medical science, discovering fantastic vaccines and developing almost unbelievable surgical skills. We've conquered many natural laws, developing radio, television, jet power, missile systems, and computer technology. We've even put men on the moon and brought them safely back to earth. Who knows what we still may accomplish with the "information highway" and traveling through space?

The facts are that without God's help, we could have accomplished none of these things. A Christian man knows this to be true—and acknowledges it! He doesn't deny that God has used him, his abilities, his talents, and his skills, as well as his ability to believe that he can accomplish great things with these capabilities. But a true Christian man also knows that it is God who gives each of us the strength and energy to succeed in life. When all is said and done, a mature Christian man accepts honor when honor is due, but always gives ultimate glory to God!

Principle 2. As men, we'll always have the challenge of maintaining a proper perspective regarding ourselves in relationship to our fellow men.

We live in a world of competition. From the time we begin playing Little League sports, we've been brainwashed into thinking that public acceptance and approval is based on winning. As we grow older, we discover the same thing is true in school—and eventually in business.

How can we practice the principle of servanthood yet compete? Jesus said it's possible—if we practice His teachings and follow His example. It's not wrong to be a leader. It's not wrong to achieve goals that in some instances keep others from achieving the same goals. But the Scriptures clearly outline how this should happen. We're to always maintain a servant mentality, even when we are more successful than others and have greater positions. The more responsibility we have, the greater servants we are to become! Jesus demonstrated this beautifully when He washed the disciples' feet (John 13:12–13).

Paul also outlines a strategy that should characterize every Christian man (and woman): "Do nothing out of selfish ambition or vain conceit, but in humility consider others better than yourselves. Each of you should look not only to your own interests, but also to the interests of others" (Phil. 2:3–4).

It's not wrong to have our "own interests." It's a fact of life. But if we maintain the same attitude as Jesus Christ (2:6–8), we'll be able to balance "our own interests" with a deep concern for the "interests of others." With Christ's help, it is possible to "honor others above ourselves" (Rom. 12:10)—even though we may have a greater position and more responsibility.

Principle 3. As men, we'll always face the challenge to avoid those moments of opportunism that will bring glory to ourselves rather than to God and others.

There's a great difference between being an "opportunist" and using to the full the "opportunities" that come our way. An opportunist is always looking for ways to gain an advantage over someone else. He focuses on self-promotion and self-advancement. An opportunist is usually not concerned about anyone but himself—and what he can get. It's a self-centered approach to life.

A man who takes advantage of opportunities can do so to glorify God. In fact, we're usually complacent and perhaps lazy if we do not walk through the doors that open in front of us. It's not even wrong to create opportunities.

But, again, it's how we go about it! It's a matter of focus. It's operating out of a spirit of love and avoiding anything that is unethical. And when we succeed in using every opportunity, we are to use those achievements as an opportunity to help others. With Christ's help and following His example, we can "be successful" without violating Christian principles. But the line is thin, and we must be on guard against living more for ourselves than for God and others.

Personalizing These Principles

The following questions will help you personalize these principles. As you read them, ask the Holy Spirit to pinpoint any areas in your life in which you are violating these biblical guidelines.

1. How often do I use the little words "I" and "me" in my conversations with God and with others?

   [Note: You may need to solicit the help from another Christian brother to help you evaluate whether or not you have a balance in using first person pronouns.]

2. On the other hand, am I characterized by "false humility"—trying to give the impression I am honoring God and others but merely camouflaging my motives and actions with my words?

3. How often do I use the words "thank you" when talking to God and others?

4. How often are God and others in my thoughts, compared with thoughts about myself?

5. How well am I able to handle "success" as well as "failure"?

Set a Goal

As you reflect on the answers to these questions in the light of the principles outlined above, what one goal do you feel you need to set for your life?

_____

_____

_____

_____

Memorize the Following Scripture

Now to him who is able to do immeasurably more than all we ask or imagine, according to his power that is at work within us, to him be glory in the church and in Christ Jesus throughout all generations for ever and ever! Amen.
                                                EPH. 3:20–21

Growing Together

1. When are we as men most vulnerable to pride?

2. What steps can we take to maintain a proper balance between realizing that we've been able to accomplish things in life because of self-discipline and self-determination, and yet give praise and glory to God?

3. How can we avoid "false humility"?

4. How can we avoid projecting our own struggles with pride onto our fellow men?

5. How can we pray for you specifically?

Chapter 7

A Dynamic Lesson in Management
Read Exodus 18:1–27

*H*ave you ever been so overwhelmed with problems and responsibilities that you couldn't see your way out? Moses faced this dilemma in the wilderness. But God used a man—a very unexpected person—to give him a solution.

Following the Cloud

Once across the Red Sea, Moses led the children of Israel southward into the wilderness, not by choice, but by God's direction. Choosing the northern route would have been more logical, especially in view of the mass of humanity who would soon need food and water, not only for themselves but also for their herds and flocks. But the "cloud" moved southward (Exod. 13:17–22). After his great declaration to God's sovereign leadership in his song of victory, Moses was not about to take matters into his own hands. He had learned too much about God's presence and power in his life.

But Moses' "wilderness school" experience was just beginning, and little did he realize how much more he was going to learn about being an effective leader. True, he had come a long way. Psychologically, God had step by step rebuilt his self-image. And spiritually, Moses had learned to trust God. It was the well-learned lessons in faith that enabled Moses to lead this great hoard of people directly into the wilderness, a maneuver that by human standards would be classified as irrational, foolish, and irresponsible. The author of Hebrews testifies to this spiritual dynamic in Moses' life: "*By faith* he left Egypt, not fearing the king's anger; he persevered because he saw him who is invisible. *By faith* he kept the Passover and the sprinkling of blood, so that the destroyer of the firstborn would not touch the firstborn of Israel. *By faith* the people passed through the Red Sea as on dry land; but when the Egyptians tried to do so, they were drowned" (Heb. 11:27–29).

An Awesome Task

Imagine leading a mass of people the size of a major American city into a wild and desolate desert, a wilderness where the natural resources for providing food and water were almost nonexistent. How could Moses provide for two million people —as well as their livestock?

Bitter Water at Marah

To make matters worse, the children of Israel were for the most part pagan and carnal, which became all too obvious only three days after they had left Egypt. They began to murmur and complain because the water supply at Marah was so bitter they couldn't drink it (Exod. 15:22–24). But Moses had learned a dynamic lesson. Immediately, he "cried out to the LORD"! In turn the Lord answered his prayer and "showed him a piece of wood." Moses "threw it into the water," and it "became sweet" (15:25).

No Food in the Desert

Several weeks later, in spite of God's miraculous and marvelous provision at Marah, the children of Israel were actually wishing that they "had died by the LORD's hand in Egypt" rather than to be free from their bondage (16:1–3). They had no food, but once again God met their need, providing

them with manna from heaven. Every day for forty years, God
provided them with food—in spite of their frequent disobedience (16:1–36).

No Water at Rephidim

We see God's patience and provision for the people once
again at Rephidim. This time they had no water whatsoever.
How quickly they forgot what had happened at Marah! Again
they complained and even "quarreled with Moses" (17:2).
They got so angry they threatened to stone the very man who
had led them out of Egypt. But God in his grace came to the
rescue and answered Moses' cry for help. He instructed his
servant to take his rod—probably a reminder of the Red Sea
experience—and ordered him to strike a rock. Miraculously,
water flowed in abundance (17:6).

The Amalekite Attack

Before Israel left Rephidim, God gave them another
miraculous victory over their enemies. The Amalekites
attacked, threatening to wipe them out! How could this group
of ill-equipped people survive a well-equipped army? God
used a young man named Joshua to defeat the Amalekites—a
young lieutenant who had served Moses "from his youth"
(Num. 11:28). However, it was a supernatural victory. As long
as Aaron, Moses' brother, and Hur (the Jewish historian
Josephus believed this was Miriam's husband) held up Moses'
hands, the children of Israel prevailed. Finally at sunset, "Joshua
overcame the Amalekite army with the sword" (17:13).

Reaching the "Mount of God"

One of Moses' greatest lessons in working with people came
sometime later—after he had returned with the children of
Israel to the very place God had first spoken to him from a
burning bush. The place was Mount Horeb, designated as the

"*mountain of God*" (3:1; 18:5). Here Israel set up camp and settled in.

At some point in time after Moses had returned to Egypt, he had sent his wife, Zipporah, and his two sons, Gershom and Eliezer, back to the place in which he had lived for forty years (18:2–4). Jethro had heard what Moses had done for the children of Israel and had tracked their journey through the wilderness. When they arrived at Mount Horeb, he went out to meet him bringing along his wife and sons (18:5–6).

A Miraculous Conversion

Though Jethro had heard generally about God's miraculous intervention for Israel, Moses soon filled him in on the particulars (18:8). Jethro's response to Moses' report must have been as rewarding to Moses as some of the great miracles he had observed on the way from Egypt to Mount Horeb. The miracle that Moses observed in his father-in-law's life was what the other miracles were all about: to demonstrate to those who do not know God that He is God. In short, it appears that Jethro was converted. He, like Abraham of old, put his faith in God as the one true God and the only Savior of mankind. And it was by faith in God that Jethro, too, was justified and made righteous in God's sight.

The Scriptures record that when Jethro heard about "everything the LORD had done to Pharaoh and the Egyptians for Israel's sake" (18:8), he was "delighted" (18:9). He blessed the Lord and testified: "Now I know that the LORD is greater than all other gods" (18:11). And the final step in his conversion experience—actually the confirmation—was an act of worship. He offered a burnt offering and sacrifice to the one true God (18:12).

An Insightful Observation

The day following his reunion with Moses and his conversion to God, Jethro watched Moses' activity as leader of

Israel. All day long his son-in-law dealt with problems that existed among the people of Israel. One after another they came to Moses to get advice and counsel on how to solve their personal, family, and social crises (Exod. 18:13–16). By the end of the day Moses was exhausted, and many of the Israelites were still frustrated because they had been standing in line all day long without an opportunity to get answers to their questions.

Jethro was very concerned for both Moses and the children of Israel. "'What you are doing is not good,'" he said. "'You and these people who come to you will only wear yourselves out. The work is too heavy for you; *you cannot handle it alone*'" (18:17–18).

What a significant contrast! Sometime before—in this very area—God had patiently but persistently communicated with Moses from a burning bush, attempting to convince him that He wanted Moses—and him alone—to lead Israel out of Egypt. And when Moses refused to respond to God's call, the Lord reluctantly provided him with Aaron to be his spokesman and assistant. As we've seen, God later helped Moses to rebuild his self-image and to become the sole leader of Israel, the one who took full responsibility for their leadership out of Egypt.

Moses learned that lesson well. But now he was still trying to do the job of leading Israel all by himself. At this juncture, he had another significant lesson to learn. His experience in Egypt had been a much different situation, calling for a different style of leadership. Utilizing others to help him communicate with Pharaoh was not God's plan. Furthermore, God wanted to exalt Moses, to build his image in the sight of both the Egyptians and Israel in order to prepare him for the great task of leading Israel out of Egypt and into the promised land.

But leading two million people through an uncharted wilderness called for a new style of leadership. Holding his hand in the air and waving his staff over the people of Israel was not God's plan for solving their social and interpersonal problems. It has never been God's strategy to work this way with people. Moses had to learn how to handle this new leadership role, and his newly converted father-in-law was God's instrument for communicating that new lesson.

A Practical Suggestion

Jethro's suggestion to Moses was brilliant. It had three facets. First, he suggested that Moses *serve as a mediator* between the people and God. This was to be his primary responsibility, his priority. He was to spend time seeking God's will for the people (Exod. 18:19).

Second, once Moses determined God's will, he was to *communicate* it to the people. "Then," said Jethro, "'teach them the decrees and laws, and show them the way to live and the duties they are to perform'" (18:20).

Third, he was to *delegate responsibility to qualified men* who could help him solve the day-by-day problems: "'But select *capable men* from all the people—men who *fear God, trustworthy men who hate dishonest gain*—and appoint them as officials over thousands, hundreds, fifties and tens'" (18:21).

These newly appointed leaders were to handle the normal problems—the minor matters—and only the major crises were to be brought to Moses for his wisdom and counsel (18:22–23). "'If you do this and God so commands,'" concluded Jethro, "'you will be able to stand the strain, and all these people will go home satisfied.'"

The Plan Worked

Moses had learned another significant lesson in his growth toward maturity—a lesson in management. He followed through on his father-in-law's suggestion (18:24–27). The plan worked. In fact, the organizational structure that emerged to solve their social problems also became a very workable plan for thwarting military attacks from their enemies.

Though God desired to use Moses, and him alone, in Egypt and in leading His people across the sea until they reached Mount Horeb, his plan from that point forward was to be shared responsibility. Moses learned that social problems are usually not resolved miraculously. Rather, they are solved through careful and painstaking communication and counseling. And Moses also learned that it is impossible for one man alone to do this kind of job.

Becoming God's Man Today

Principles to Live By

There are many lessons that all Christian men can learn from this unusual experience in Moses' life. Let's look at just four.

Principle 1. Management ability is a mark of spiritual maturity, and we must all develop this quality of life to be in the will of God.

In 1 Timothy 3 and Titus 1, Paul lists the marks of a mature man of God. One of those marks is management ability. Note that a man who is seeking a leadership position in the church must be someone who can "manage his own family well and see that his children obey him with proper respect." Paul then adds, "If anyone does not know how to manage his own family, how can he take care of God's church?" (1 Tim. 3:4–5).

Paul was not referring to a spiritual gift. If he were, what can men do who are fathers if they don't have the "gift of management"? How could they be effective in leading their families? Rather, Paul was referring to a skill and quality of life all men can and must develop in order to be effective fathers and effective church leaders. This characteristic is a mark of spiritual growth and maturity. With God's help, all of us can develop it.

Principle 2. We must establish priorities in all aspects of our lives to be good fathers, effective church leaders, and successful businessmen.

There are too many demands upon us to be able to do everything *and* do it well. This was Moses' problem. It was utterly impossible for him to do everything by himself. He had to establish priorities.

As with Moses, there are significant priorities that we must establish to be in the will of God:

We must not neglect our relationship with God. God's plan in order for that relationship to grow and mature is that we have three vital experiences: learning the Word of God, communing with God (worship) and with other believers (fellowship), and sharing Christ with those who do not know Him (Acts 2:42–47). It is only as we engage in these New Testament experiences that we will become mature in Christ, both as individuals and as a body.

We must not neglect our families. Our relationship with God, other believers, and non-Christians should never replace or become a substitute for leading our families into the same kind of experiences. The Word of God is clear regarding our responsibility to our families (1 Tim. 5:8).

We must not neglect our business responsibilities. There is no place in the Christian life for neglecting to be a good steward of our time when working for others. Again, listen to Paul: "Whatever you do, work at it with all your heart, as working for the Lord, not for men, since you know that you will receive an inheritance from the Lord as a reward" (Col. 3:23–24).

We must not neglect ourselves. This may seem selfish, but it may be the greatest gift you can give your family—and the Lord. Even Jesus told the disciples to not neglect themselves. "'Come with me by yourselves to a quiet place,'" He said, "'and get some rest'" (Mark 6:31).

When I was a student at Moody Bible Institute, one of my professors told this story. Two men challenged each other to a dog sled race across the great north land—a race that would take a number of weeks. After six days, one man rested his dogs while the other continued on. However, by the end of the second week, the man who had rested his dogs nearly caught up with the man who had not stopped. But once again, the first man rested his dogs on the seventh day. By the end of the third week, he not only caught up with the other team but passed them. Several weeks later when the race ended, the first man reached his destination far ahead of the man who had never stopped to rest his dogs.

I'll never forget this story. It illustrates a principle which God established in the original creation and also helped me to establish some new priorities. It's not surprising that when I take my "day off" I accomplish more in the ensuing days.

Principle 3. We must always delegate responsibility to qualified individuals.

This is a truth that appears again and again throughout the Scriptures, particularly in the appointment of leaders. Imagine what would have happened if Moses had selected immature men to help him, men who were not trustworthy. They would have multiplied his problems a thousandfold. This is why Paul puts such a strong emphasis on appointing men to church leadership who measure up to certain standards of maturity.

We must understand, of course, that no one is perfect. No Christian has "arrived" in his Christian life. But there is a recognizable level of maturity. Otherwise Paul would not have set forth those qualities in 1 Timothy 3 and Titus 1 as a criteria for measuring maturity.[1]

Principle 4. No matter what our spiritual maturity, we must always be open to advice and counsel.

At this point in his life, Moses had become a very mature man of God, both psychologically and spiritually. But there was yet more to learn. And it took a "Jethro," a new believer but a very experienced man, to help him learn a very significant lesson regarding how to become a better leader.

No Christian must ever get to the place where he is unteachable. If he does, he has ceased to be mature. There is always more to learn about God's plan for our lives—and lessons often come from very unexpected sources.

This leads to another significant reflection of maturity in Moses' life. As we've all experienced, the most difficult people to receive advice from are often those closest to us, those within our own family structure. Moses demonstrated true humility when he listened objectively to his father-in-law and followed what proved to be expert advice.

Personalizing These Principles

Select the areas in your life you believe you need to give more attention to in order to become a more mature Christian:

- ❏ Developing my management abilities in my home, in the church, and in the business world

- ❏ Establishing better priorities

- ❏ Learning to delegate responsibility to qualified people

- ❏ Being open to advice and counsel from any source God wants to use

Set a Goal

As you reflect on the principles in this chapter, use the process you've just gone through to isolate areas of need in your life. Ask the Holy Spirit to help you formulate a specific goal that you would like to begin to achieve immediately:

_____

_____

_____

_____

Memorize the Following Scripture

You are witnesses, and so is God, of how holy, righteous and blameless we were among you who believed. For you know that we dealt with each of you as a father deals with his own children, encouraging, comforting and urging you to live lives worthy of God, who calls you into his kingdom and glory.

1 THESS. 2:10–12

Growing Together

1. What is the most important lesson you've learned from this chapter?

2. Why do we need to apply the principles we've learned from Moses' experience, no matter what our leadership role? Can you give us a specific illustration?

3. How have you attempted to apply these principles in your own life? What happened when you have applied them? What happens when you don't?

4. How can we pray for you specifically?

Chapter 8

An Incredible Act of Love
Read Exodus 32:1–35

*S*uppose your grown children are guilty of gross sin: pagan idolatry and public immorality. They have ignored everything you've taught them about God's laws and principles. While you and your wife were out of the city attending a Bible and prayer conference, they turned your home into a den of iniquity. They invited a group of Satan worshippers to construct an altar in your living room. A group of psychic readers took over the family room. Every room in the house was occupied with people committing a variety of sexual acts—both heterosexual and homosexual. Every television set was playing X-rated videos. Your own bedroom was being used to conduct a seance where witches were attempting to communicate with the dead!

How would you feel if God suddenly appeared to you on your trip, told you what was happening, and then informed you He was so angry that He was going to destroy all of your children, their spouses, your grandchildren—and all the friends they had invited to your home for this wild experience? What would you do? Would you be willing to die for them—and have your own name blotted out of the Book of Life if God spared them?

If you say "yes" to this final question, you would be doing what Moses did when the children of Israel built a golden calf, worshiped it, and committed gross immorality at the foot of Mount Sinai. This was an incredible act of love—and the greatest test Moses ever faced! Few of us, if any, would be willing to pay this price.

Indescribable Degradation

Long before Israel was delivered from Egyptian bondage, the world was almost totally given over to idolatry and immorality. All mankind had forsaken the Lord. The downward process of spiritual degeneration and deterioration, which the apostle Paul described so graphically in his letter to the Romans, and which once resulted in the flood, had once again taken place.

Men, who at one time "knew God . . . neither glorified him as God" and "their thinking became futile and their foolish hearts were darkened." Eventually, they "exchanged the glory of the immortal God for images made to look like mortal man and birds and animals and reptiles." Correlated with this deterioration came another predictable phenomenon— flagrant immorality. Consequently, "God gave them over in the sinful desires of their hearts to sexual impurity for the degrading of their bodies with one another." Not only did they engage in heterosexual sins, but homosexual sins—which Paul described as "shameful lusts" (Rom. 1:21–27).

Unfathomable Grace

Though the whole world had turned against God, He began the process of redemption by choosing Abraham and his wife, Sarah, out of the pagan masses. He made Abraham three promises: that He would give him and his descendants *a land*, that He would make him *a great nation*, and that through him all the families of the earth would experience *a wonderful blessing* (Gen. 12:1–3). These promises were repeated to Abraham in the presence of his son, Isaac (22:15–18), and to Isaac's son, Jacob (28:13–14)—who in turn had twelve sons. These twelve sons were the men who gave birth to the nation Israel who multiplied greatly when they settled in Egypt. When Moses led them out, they had already become a great nation.

God cannot lie, no matter how fickle, dishonest, and immoral man becomes—including His own people. In leading them out of Egypt, God was in the process of also keeping His first promise—to give them the land of Canaan.

When Israel arrived at Mount Sinai, God took His most loving and compassionate step. He revealed Himself to Israel directly: first, through lightning, thunder, smoke, fire, and the sound of the trumpet. In fact, the "whole mountain trembled violently" (Exod. 19:18). In the midst of this awe-inspiring phenomenon, they all heard God's voice (19:9).

First, God told His people that it was He who had brought them out of the land of Egypt (20:1–2). He then gave them ten clear-cut commandments, and it was not an afterthought that the first commandment condemned idolatry. "'You shall have no other gods before Me,'" said Jehovah. "'You shall not make for yourself an idol in the form of anything in heaven above or on the earth beneath or in the waters below. You shall not bow down to them or worship them" (20:3–5, 18–19, 22).

During Israel's stay at Mount Sinai, Moses ascended the mountain numerous times and entered the very presence of God to receive additional instructions regarding the way the children of Israel should worship the Lord and how they should treat each other (chapters 20–24). On one occasion, Moses stayed forty days and nights to receive God's instructions for erecting the Tabernacle (chapters 25–31). It was during this time that many in Israel—in the full light of God's power, holiness, love, grace, care, and concern—reverted to almost incredible idolatry and immorality. They flagrantly violated the first commandment!

Unbelievable Ingratitude

The children of Israel demonstrate that all of us are inherently selfish and capable of the worst kinds of ungrateful behavior.

They also illustrate how difficult it is to change sinful patterns, especially when those patterns have been a pervasive and permanent part of our lives. But for most of us, they prove how short our memories really are when it comes to remembering God's grace and mercy.

The Miracles in Egypt

Think for a moment what God had already done for Israel. They had witnessed the powerful signs God had given to Moses (4:29–30). They had experienced the ten plagues in Egypt and God's protective hand in the midst of these violent demonstrations of His wrath and power (7:14–12:30). They had walked through the Red Sea on dry ground and then looked on with amazement as God destroyed the Egyptians in the midst of the sea (14:21–31).

Miracles in the Wilderness

During the wilderness journey to Sinai, the children of Israel had heard Moses cry to the Lord on their behalf at Marah and then drank the bitter water that turned sweet (15:22–25). They had been eating the quail that God sent every evening, and continued to gather the manna that God sent every morning (16:1–36).

While at Rephidim, they had seen Moses strike a rock with his rod and had witnessed pure, cool water gush out (17:1–7). In that very place, they had also experienced a supernatural victory over Amalek and his people because Moses had held his hands toward heaven—a reminder from God how He had used His servant's rod and hands on previous occasions to deliver them from Egypt (17:8–16).

Miracles at Sinai

God's most powerful manifestation happened at Sinai. His people had already seen the mountain quake, accompanied by lightning, thunder, fire, smoke, and the sound of the trumpet (19:16–19). They had literally heard the voice of God warning them against worshiping false gods(19:9; 20:1–6). And, on several occasions, they had witnessed Moses ascend and descend the mountain, entering the cloud to receive instructions from God. In fact, just before Moses had entered the cloud to stay for forty days and nights, seventy elders of Israel—with Aaron and his sons—went up the mountain with Moses and saw a literal manifestation of God Himself (24:9–11).

What an awesome experience this must have been! It's inconceivable that the children of Israel at this moment would turn their backs on God. But they did! They spurned God's grace and engaged in unbelievable idolatry and immorality.

Incredible Rebellion

Moses entered the presence of God and withdrew from Israel's sight for only six weeks. Sometime during this period, the people grew restless. Their leader had disappeared, and they began to doubt God's presence and power—which in itself defies explanation. The fiery cloud was still there. They were eating the miraculous manna every morning. And what is more amazing, only a couple of weeks had gone by since they had heard God speak from the smoking mountain. How could their memories be so short?

Nevertheless, they convinced Aaron to fashion the image of a "god" made with human hands from their own material possessions, a "god" they could see and worship. And what is more difficult to understand is that Aaron succumbed to their demands to make this "graven image" (32:1–6). How could he do this in view of his own experience as he stood by Moses' side during those miraculous manifestations in Egypt? God actually allowed Aaron to work some of these miracles. Could it be that he was overcome with pride and wanted to maintain his position of power and prominence? Or was it fear of what these people might do to him? Whatever his motivation, his participation in this act of rebellion also defies explanation.

We must understand that with this terrible act of sin, Israel was not denying God's existence and substituting a "god" in His place. Rather, they wanted a "representative" of this God of Abraham, Isaac, and Jacob—a "god" that they could see and touch. Moses had disappeared. During his absence, they wanted an "animal" in which the God who led them out of Egypt would dwell. This was a reversion to the pagan practices they had learned in Egypt.

Here also is an ancient illustration of how easy and "natural" it is for people raised in a pagan environment to mix pagan religious practices with true religious practices. We call this syncretism. This is happening in many parts of the world today, particularly in Central and South America where demonic, pagan, and Christian symbols are all blended together to create a mixture of truth and error. My wife and I have personally witnessed a Christian cross in a witch's cave. The floor of the cave was covered with the remains of animal sacrifices—bones, feathers, chicken feed, etc.

How could God's people devise such a plan, especially in view of the Lord's repeated warnings regarding the danger of even approaching the mountain because of His great holiness and majesty (19:21–24). But they did! They created a golden calf and offered sacrifices to this graven image. They ate and drank as part of their religious ritual, and engaged in open and degrading immorality—a reflection of what they had learned and practiced in Egypt. Immoral behavior became a part of their religious worship (1 Cor. 10:7–8).

Righteous Indignation

The Lord's reaction to Israel's abominable actions is explicitly recorded in the Scriptures: "'I have seen this people,' the LORD said to Moses, 'and they are a stiff-necked people. Now leave me alone so that my anger may burn against them and that I may destroy them'" (Exod. 32:9–10a).

God had run out of patience. In view of all that he had done to help Israel—by revealing His power, teaching them His laws, and demonstrating His love and care—He was now so disgusted with their flagrant rejection that He was ready to wipe them off the face of the earth.

At this point, we see Moses' greatest test—and his greatest act of love. The Lord told Moses He was ready to start over, to destroy all of these people He had brought out of Egypt and then to fulfill His promises to Abraham through Moses and his immediate family. "'Then I will make *you* into a great nation,'" God said (32:10b).

What a temptation this would be for Moses—an opportunity to become the center of human history and to be free from the responsibility to lead this rebellious mass of humanity. After all, this was God's idea, not his! Furthermore, these people had also rejected Moses. He had given up his position in Egypt to lead them out of slavery. Why *not* start over—and with God's blessing? At this moment, the Lord removed every human and divine roadblock for Moses. He could not rationalize his behavior if he wanted to. He had every honest reason a man needs to cooperate with this plan. God was not playing games with Moses.

Supernatural Compassion

Moses' maturity and love is overwhelming, especially in view of his previous spiritual and psychological weaknesses. He immediately interceded for the children of Israel (32:11). Pleading with the Lord on their behalf, He reminded God of His original purpose in bringing these people out from bondage—to demonstrate His great power before the Egyptians (32:12). He also reminded the Lord of His promise to Abraham, Isaac, and Jacob (32:13).

This event more than any other demonstrates Moses' spiritual growth since that day God spoke to him from the burning bush. His love for Israel is beyond description. A couple of years before, he was not even willing to leave the wilderness to help deliver them from bondage. Now we see him pleading with God to save them. He even offered to spend eternity separated from God if He would restrain His wrath (32:32). Neither was Moses playing games with God. He meant what he said.

Through this direct and open communication with the Lord, Moses changed God's mind—something no one can explain in human terms. We read that "the LORD relented [changed His mind] and did not bring on his people the disaster he had threatened" (32:14).

Evidently God did not reveal His change of plans to Moses immediately. He allowed him to go down to the people and to confront them with their sin. Moses was so angry at what he saw that "he threw the tablets out of his hands, breaking them to pieces at the foot of the mountain" (32:19). He then destroyed the golden calf, grinding "it to powder" and scattering it in Israel's water supply (32:20). Moses then confronted Aaron with his irresponsibility.

Mind-boggling Rationalization

Aaron's reaction to Moses' confrontation would be humorous if it were not so tragic! He rationalized his behavior and blamed the people—a classic example of our tendency toward self-deception and dishonesty. The dialogue between Moses and his brother was intense and emotional: "He said to Aaron, 'What did these people do to you, that you led them into such great sin?' 'Do not be angry, my lord,' Aaron answered. 'You know how prone these people are to evil. They said to me, "Make us gods who will go before us. As for this fellow Moses who brought us up out of Egypt, we don't know what has happened to him." So I told them, "Whoever has any gold jewelry, take it off." Then they gave me the gold, and I threw it into the fire, *and out came this calf!*'" (32:21–24).

"Out came this calf!" What an incredible example of a guilty man with his back against the wall! The truth is, Aaron had deliberately taken the golden ornaments the people gave him and used a special tool to make an idol into "the shape of a calf" (32:3–4). Aaron purposely and willingly cooperated with their request to construct this false god and consequently was just as guilty as they were of flagrant idolatry.

Gracious Restoration

Holding Aaron responsible, Moses set out immediately to restore order among the children of Israel—who had become a laughingstock to their enemies (32:25). He confronted the debauchery and sordid behavior that existed throughout the camp. And once he had done as much "damage control" as possible (32:26–29), he again ascended the holy mountain to plead Israel's case, to try to change God's mind, and to see if he could make atonement for their sins (32:30–31). In His sovereignty, the Lord had already decided to punish only those who were guilty (32:33–34). But at this point, Moses did not understand God's "change of mind." He was deadly serious about making atonement for Israel with his own life.

Moses' approach to God on Israel's behalf is an overwhelming lesson in pastoral love and concern. His actions defy all human explanation, for he made it clear to the Lord that he wanted to die with his people if they were not spared. "'But now, please forgive their sin—'" he pleaded, "'but if not, then blot me out of the book you have written'" (32:32).

Becoming God's Man Today

Principles to Live By

What we've just learned from Moses takes us into the eternal and divine dimension—God's unfathomable love and justice! It's indescribable and beyond our comprehension

(Rom. 11:33–36). But it's still true that God wants us to love others because He first loved us (1 John 4:19). In fact, it's God's love for us that enables us to love at all.

Principle 1. No man can love as Moses loved apart from God's supernatural power and grace.

I know of only one other human example of the kind of love Moses demonstrated toward the children of Israel. When Paul wrote to the Romans, he spoke from a heart of compassion that is beyond explanation: "I speak the truth in Christ—I am not lying, my conscience confirms it in the Holy Spirit—I have great sorrow and unceasing anguish in my heart. For I could wish that I myself were cursed and cut off from Christ for the sake of my brothers, those of my own race, the people of Israel" (Rom. 9:1–4a).

In actuality, God has never asked any man to pay this price! Neither would He approve or accept this arrangement—just as he stopped Abraham from offering his son Isaac (Gen. 22:12). However, the fact that both Moses and Paul were willing to be cursed for the sake of their people demonstrates supernatural grace. It's impossible to love this way apart from God's eternal presence and power in our lives!

However, there *is* a love that God asks us to demonstrate toward our fellow Christians. It *does* involve a willingness to die! John explains it clearly in his first epistle: "This is how we know what love is: Jesus Christ laid down his life for us. And we ought to lay down our lives for our brothers" (1 John 3:16).

Tradition tells us that all of the apostles, except John, gave their lives as martyrs. They literally died that others could come to know the Lord Jesus Christ as Savior. This is what Paul meant when he wrote to the Thessalonians: "We loved you so much that we were delighted to share with you not only the gospel of God *but our lives as well,* because you had become so dear to us" (1 Thess. 2:8).

Most of us—thank God—will never be faced with the decision to go this far in demonstrating love. Many Christians have over the years. But this raises a very practical question. What *are* we willing to do to demonstrate love to another brother?

Before we talk about dying for one another, we need to ask ourselves if we're willing to "walk across the street" for our brother.

Paul gives us good criteria for evaluating our motives in the letter he wrote to the Corinthians. This is how he defined the love we should demonstrate toward our fellow believers:

- Love is patient,
    love is kind.
- It does not envy,
    it does not boast,
    it is not proud.
- It is not rude,
    it is not self-seeking,
    it is not easily angered,
    it keeps no record of wrongs.
- Love does not delight in evil
    but rejoices with the truth.
- It always protects,
    always trusts,
    always hopes,
    always perseveres (1 Cor. 13:4–7).

Are you willing to demonstrate this kind of love toward another brother (or sister) in Christ?

Principle 2. We must always be on guard against taking God's love and grace for granted.

Generally, mankind has always been fickle. The history of the human race is one of taking God for granted and eventually turning away from Him. The children of Israel, God's chosen people, have fallen into this trap again and again throughout their own history. In this chapter, we've looked at an almost unbelievable illustration of this reality. Sadly, the book of Judges is a cyclical saga of Israel's idolatry, God's judgment, and then Israel's repentance and restoration.

But as Christians, we are often guilty as well. How easy it is to forget God's blessings! How short our memories are when it comes to remembering what God has done for us in the past! How quickly we complain when things don't go just the way we want them to! How easy it is to feel sorry for ourselves, even in the midst of material and spiritual blessings that surround us on every side. And how easy it is to rationalize our behavior, like Aaron—to engage in irresponsible behavior and to deny our guilt!

As Christians, we are not disciplined by law but by grace. Unfortunately, it's easy to take advantage of that grace. To what extent do you understand God's mercy and grace? To what degree are you allowing that grace to mold your life into the image of Jesus Christ? The apostle Paul understood this grace—which is a powerful lesson for all of us: "For the grace of God that brings salvation has appeared to all men. It teaches us to say 'no' to ungodliness and worldly passions, and to live self-controlled, upright and godly lives in this present age, while we wait for the blessed hope—the glorious appearing of our great God and Savior, Jesus Christ, who gave himself for us to redeem us from all wickedness and to purify for himself a people that are his very own, eager to do what is good" (Titus 2:11–14).

Principle 3. Jesus Christ is the only one who has demonstrated God's love to the fullest degree, and He wants to implant that love in our hearts through His indwelling Holy Spirit.

Moses' love for Israel is a beautiful illustration of what Jesus Christ did for us when He came into this world to be our Savior. He took upon Himself our guilt and bore it on the cross. He experienced temporary separation from God so that we might not experience eternal separation.

It's the ultimate ingratitude for a Christian to ignore this kind of love and to "indulge the sinful nature" rather than to live "by the Spirit" (Gal. 5:13–16).

On one occasion, a Pharisee came to Jesus and asked Him which was "'the greatest commandment in the Law.'" Jesus' answer is powerful and penetrating:

""'Love the Lord your God with all your heart and with all your soul and with all your mind." This is the first and greatest commandment. And the second is like it: "Love your neighbor as yourself." All the Law and the Prophets hang on these two commandments'" (Matt. 22:37–39).

We cannot satisfactorily conclude this study without mentioning another wonderful truth that must be added to Christ's command to love God and others. He has not asked us to do this in our own strength. He is willing and waiting to empower us with His Holy Spirit. Paul made this point clearly in his letter to the Romans:

"God has poured out his love into our hearts by the Holy Spirit, whom he has given us" (Rom. 5:5).

Personalizing These Principles

The following questions will help you evaluate your life and the degree to which you are applying the principles outlined in this chapter:

1. To what extent are you loving others as Christ loved you— your wife, your children, your brothers and sisters in Christ?

2. To what extent are you taking God's love and grace for granted by living a self-centered and carnal life?

3. Have you received God's wonderful gift of love—the gift of eternal life? (Eph. 2:8–9). If so, are you allowing

the Holy Spirit to empower you to love others as He has loved us?

Set a Goal

Use the above questions and principles to evaluate your Christian experience. As you do, ask the Holy Spirit to pinpoint one area in your life that you need to give immediate attention to. Then write out a goal:

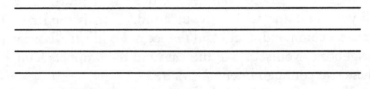

Memorize the Following Scripture

Commit the following Scripture to memory in order to help you realize your goal:

> *You, my brothers, were called to be free. But do not use your freedom to indulge the sinful nature; rather, serve one another in love. The entire law is summed up in a single command: "Love your neighbor as yourself."*
> GALATIANS 5:13–14

Growing Together

1. Why is it so difficult to think about others before we think about ourselves?

2. Why is it so easy to take God's love and grace for granted? Would you feel free to share how this has happened in your own life?

3. Would you be willing to share one area in your own life where you want to be more diligent in practicing God's love?

4. How can we pray for you specifically?

Chapter 9

Face to Face with God
Read Exodus 33:1–34:17

*H*enry Blackaby has written an excellent and heart-warming book entitled *Experiencing God.* The title in itself speaks volumes, since oftentimes reading and studying the Scriptures can be an academic experience—an experience in learning *about God* and how He works rather than an experience *with God* and how He wants to be a part of our lives.

Don't misunderstand. The Bible *is* historical! It is a factual record of how God has worked in the lives of His people. But when we read it, it should be more. The Holy Spirit, who authored the Bible through human hands, wants us to get beyond factual information and come to know God better, to experience more of His character, His love, and His grace!

What Moses experienced next is the kind of event that touches our hearts—not just our heads. As I reviewed this section of Scripture, I was deeply touched in my own heart. I found myself wanting to know God better, to be able to communicate with Him as if He were "my friend" too! You see, He *is* my friend—and yours too if you know Him personally as your Heavenly Father. You *can* know Him in this way if you have received His Son, the Lord Jesus Christ, as your personal Savior. Jesus Christ is the one who has made it possible for you and me to enter into God's eternal presence—any moment of any day.

But I'm beginning where I want to end! What *was* Moses' experience? Why is this next event in his life so dynamic and challenging? In essence, we see Moses communicating with God as friends communicate—"face to face"!

A Crisis Experience

Moses' relationship with God reached a new level of intimacy because of a crisis. In the full light of God's presence and glory, the children of Israel had engaged in unbelievable idolatry—worshiping a golden calf. God became so angry He wanted to "destroy them" all—except Moses and his family. But Moses asked the Lord to spare them. If He didn't, Moses asked God to blot out his own name from the book of life. He asked to die with the children of Israel—both physically and spiritually (Exod. 32:32). This is a commitment to people that has only been superseded by Jesus Christ.

In an act of love that we can only understand by faith, the sovereign Lord of the universe relented (changed His mind) and "did not bring on his people the disaster he had threatened" (32:14). However, the Lord made it clear He could not let this sin go unpunished. He was going to remove His presence from Israel. The words God gave to Moses to relay to the children of Israel ring with a note of finality:

"'Go up to the land flowing with milk and honey. *But I will not go with you*, because you are a stiff-necked people and I might destroy you on the way'" (33:3).

In other words, God told the children of Israel He would no longer manifest Himself to them as He had done from Egypt to Sinai, working miracles and personally dwelling among them. He would not lead them with a "pillar of cloud" by day and a "pillar of fire" by night (13:21).

Again, don't misunderstand! God is omnipresent and always has been and always will be. He is everywhere. However, He has chosen at certain times in history to make

Himself known in unusual ways, to localize His presence through unusual manifestations. This He had done for Israel, especially at Sinai.

When Moses reported God's decision to Israel, they were shocked, fearful, and humbled. They "began to mourn" (33:4) and removed their ornaments as God commanded, no doubt a symbolic act of repentance for using these items to fashion a false god (33:5–6).

A Place to Meet God

Though the Lord told his people He would no longer go with them, He was still available. Before the tabernacle was ever constructed, Moses put up a tent outside the camp of Israel. There Moses would go to talk with God "face to face, as a man speaks with his friend" (33:11). The opportunity to visit this tent was also open to anyone in Israel who honestly wanted to seek God's will (33:7).

Here we see God's love and grace once again. Though He had rejected Israel as a nation, He was still available to those individuals who sincerely wanted to walk in His footsteps. This is the way it has always been, for even today, in spite of the sins of all mankind, anyone who sincerely calls upon the Lord can be saved (Rom. 10:13). God is still reaching out to individuals, no matter how much mankind in general has rejected Him.

Heart-to-Heart Communication

Moses always had a particular place in God's heart. The Lord called him to be a mediator between Israel and Himself, and as Moses faithfully discharged this responsibility, God revealed Himself to him in a unique and special way. But at this point, Moses' relationship with God deepened. Though he approached the Lord with a great sense of awe and reverence, he also shared his intense feelings of frustration and anguish. He communicated with the eternal and sovereign God of the universe in openness and candor—truly as a friend with a friend. But what is so overwhelming is that Moses influenced God's actions. The Lord listened to Moses and responded.

God had told Moses that He would be with him—not with the children of Israel—as he led them to the promised land (33:14). This was very threatening to Moses! We see this in his response to the Lord: "'If your Presence does not go with *us*, do not send us up from here'" (33:15). In other words, Moses informed the Lord he did not want to go any further if God would not be with Israel as well as with himself.

It's easy to understand Moses' thinking. If Israel had rejected God's presence and voice at Sinai, what guarantee did he have that they would follow him—even though he was in direct contact with God? In an honest and respectful way, Moses reminded the Lord that He was asking him to do the seemingly impossible. If Israel wouldn't respect God and respond to Him—the all-powerful miracle-working God of the universe—then why would they respond to a mere man? After all, they had rejected Moses all along when things got tough.

God's response to Moses was sympathetic. He listened to Moses' logic and to his plea. "'I will do the very thing you have asked,'" God responded, "'because I am pleased with you and I know you by name'" (33:17). Again, we cannot comprehend or explain how an all-knowing God can respond to a rational explanation from a human being and "change His mind." But He did!

The Glory of the Lord

With this reassuring response, Moses took another daring step. He asked the Lord to reveal His glory (33:18). He was actually asking God to allow him to look upon His face. Though Moses had been communicating with God as friends talk "face to face," he had not yet looked fully into God's face.

Unknown to him at this moment, this was impossible—for to look at God in this way, to see the very essence of His glory and personality, would be so overwhelming that Moses would die. "'You cannot see my face,'" God responded, "'for no one may see me and live'" (33:20).

The Lord then outlined an alternate plan: "'There is a place near me where you may stand on a rock. When my glory passes by, I will put you in a cleft in the rock and cover you with my hand until I have passed by. Then I will remove my hand and you will see my back; but my face must not be seen'" (33:21–23).

God then invited Moses once again to come to the top of Mount Sinai. There He revealed Himself to Moses as He said He would (34:1–8). In the midst of this glorious manifestation, Moses fell on his face and worshiped and again voiced his prayer for Israel: "'O Lord, if I have found favor in your eyes,' he said, 'then let the Lord go with us. Although this is a stiff-necked people, forgive our wickedness and our sin, and take us as your inheritance'" (34:9).

A Renewed Promise

Because of His incomprehensible love for Moses and the children of Israel, God answered His servant's prayer and renewed His covenant—but with a clear-cut stipulation. The Lord promised to be with Israel. He even promised to do more than Moses asked—to "do wonders never before done in any nation in all the world" (34:10).

However, the Lord made it very clear that He would never again tolerate Israel's idolatry (34:14–17). They must never "make a treaty with those who live in the land," otherwise, these people would become "a snare among" them (34:12). Furthermore, they must destroy the false gods of Canaan—breaking "down their altars," smashing "their sacred stones" and cutting "down their Asherah poles" (34:13). If they turned away from God again as they had done at Mount

Sinai, the Lord promised that He would bring judgment on them that was beyond their comprehension (Deut. 4:23–28).

As we know from recorded history, Israel did not follow through on their promise to be true to Jehovah. Eventually, God's judgment fell. Those in what was to become the Northern Kingdom were scattered to the ends of the earth. Those in the Southern Kingdom were taken into Babylonian captivity.

Down through history and to this very day—even after they were given a homeland in 1948—the children of Israel have been rejected and hated by many people all over the world. With every passing day and year, recurring crises in the Middle East verify this reality. However, though God has judged Israel as He said He would, this never justifies hatred and evil treatment of the Jews. In fact, those who persecute them will also experience God's judgment. Yet what has happened to the children of Israel is a part of God's prophetic plan, and someday He will restore them completely to their land and move in their hearts by His Spirit. They will then realize it was the true Messiah who died on the cross for the sins of the world (Ezek. 36:24–28; Zech. 12:10).

There is no way, of course, that we can understand these divine paradoxes; but then who has ever been able fully to comprehend the ways of the infinite, eternal God? Paul wrestled with this question and then concluded:

> Oh, the depth of the riches of
>   the wisdom and knowledge of God!
> How unsearchable his judgments,
>   and his paths beyond tracing out!
> "Who has known the mind of the Lord?
>   Or who has been his counselor?"
> "Who has ever given to God, that God should repay him?"
> For from him and through him and to him are all things.
> To him be the glory forever!
>   Amen (Rom. 11:33–36).

Becoming God's Man Today

Principles to Live By

There are some wonderful truths in this Old Testament story. As Christians, we can understand these principles and apply them with the full knowledge of what Christ has done to make it possible for us to enter the presence of God.

Principle 1. God has made it possible for all people to enter into His presence and to communicate with Him "face to face."

Today, few Christians fully realize how accessible God is to all those who know the Lord Jesus Christ as personal Savior. The author of the book of Hebrews makes this point throughout this great New Testament letter. For example, consider the following: "Therefore, since we have a great high priest who has gone through the heavens, Jesus the Son of God, let us hold firmly to the faith we profess. For we do not have a high priest who is unable to sympathize with our weaknesses, but we have one who has been tempted in every way, just as we are—yet was without sin. *Let us then approach the throne of grace with confidence,* so that we may receive mercy and find grace to help us in our time of need" (Heb. 4:14–16).

Because of Christ's death and resurrection and because of His perfect sacrifice for our sins, we can come into God's presence any time and openly and honestly pour out our concerns —just like Moses did.

As Christians, we need not go to a special place on a special day to worship God—although we are certainly commanded to gather together with other Christians on a regular basis (Heb. 10:24–25). We need not even wear special clothes, or use certain words. We need not crawl on our hands and knees and attempt to purify ourselves with certain rituals. Rather, we can worship God anywhere—at home, at school, or at work, while walking down the street, driving the car, or quarterbacking a football game. We can call out to Him at any time and under any circumstances, whether working in a bank wearing a white shirt or digging a ditch wearing overalls.

Our style of communication is not important either, for God understands simple sentences, complex sentences, big words, little words—and all languages. In fact, He understands even when we don't use words at all. Paul made this point clear in his letter to the Romans: "In the same way, the Spirit helps us in our weakness. We do not know what we ought to pray for, but the Spirit himself intercedes for us with groans that words cannot express. And he who searches our hearts knows the mind of the Spirit, because the Spirit intercedes for the saints in accordance with God's will" (Rom. 8:26–27).

Our posture is not important either. We can talk with God on our knees, with hands folded and eyes closed. Or we can talk to God standing erect, looking toward heaven, with our hands held high and our eyes wide open. We need not engage in any ritual to get God's attention.

Jesus Christ has done everything that is necessary to allow us to come into God's most holy presence. We don't need a human priest, such as a "Moses" or an "Aaron." Consequently, Paul wrote: "For there is one God and one mediator between God and men, the man Christ Jesus" (1 Tim. 2:5).

Most wonderful of all, we need not turn our faces away from God. Rather we can enter His very presence unafraid. Note again what we read in Hebrews: "Therefore, brothers, since we have confidence to enter the Most Holy Place by the blood of Jesus, by a new and living way opened for us through the curtain, that is, his body, and since we have a great priest over the house of God, *let us draw near to God* with a sincere heart in full assurance of faith, having our hearts sprinkled to cleanse us from a guilty conscience and having our bodies washed with pure water" (Heb. 10:19–22).

Principle 2. God is merciful and wants to live in constant fellowship with His children.

God's forgiveness begins with salvation. This is why Jesus Christ came. John states: "If we confess our sins, he is faithful and just and will forgive us our sins and purify us from all unrighteousness" (1 John 1:9).

All of us can experience this forgiveness when we confess our sins and receive the Lord Jesus Christ as our personal Savior. He comes to dwell in our lives and to make us a new creation (2 Cor. 5:17). In Christ, all of our sins have been paid for—past, present, and future.

From this point forward, God wants to live in constant fellowship with His children. Does this mean we need to ask for forgiveness continually in order to be forgiven? I don't believe so—but we must confess and acknowledge our sins in *order to experience the freedom there is in the "forgiveness"* that we already have in Christ. This enables us to live in constant fellowship with God. And certainly God sees beyond our rhetoric when we "ask for forgiveness" as a Christian. In His heart, He is no doubt saying, "I've already forgiven you, my child. Welcome back into fellowship with me."

On the other hand, if we continue to live in sin, God will discipline us as our loving, heavenly Father in order to bring us back into His perfect will (Heb. 12:7–11).

Personalizing These Principles

The following questions and comments will help you apply these principles in your life:

1. Have you received the Lord Jesus Christ as your personal Savior from sin? Can you pinpoint the moment when this happened?

It's true that some Christians cannot remember the specific time they confessed their sins and received the Lord Jesus Christ as their Savior, primarily because of their Christian upbringing. However, if you're not sure you're a Christian, you can make sure by receiving the Lord Jesus Christ today. The following prayer will help you—although you can use your own words:

Dear Father in heaven. I confess that I have sinned and have fallen short of your perfect standard for holy and righteous living. I thank you that the Lord Jesus Christ—the perfect Son of God— paid for my sins by dying on the cross. I now receive Him as my personal Savior from sin. Thank you for coming into my life and for saving me. In Jesus' name, Amen.

2. As a Christian, are you walking in constant fellowship with God the Father, Jesus Christ His Son, and the blessed Holy Spirit? If not, confess your sins and be restored to fellowship this very moment. Experience the wonderful forgiveness you have in Jesus Christ.

3. Are you using your glorious privilege to come into the very presence of God because of Jesus Christ your great high priest and mediator? You can get to know God better, just as Moses did. You can fellowship with Him "face to face." This is what Paul prayed for the Ephesians —and you can make this your prayer too:

I keep asking that the God of our Lord Jesus Christ, the glorious Father, may give you the Spirit of wisdom and revelation, so that you may know him better. I pray also that the eyes of your heart may be enlightened in order that you may know the hope to which he has called you, the riches of his glorious inheritance in the saints, and his incomparably great power for us who believe. . . . I pray that out of his glorious riches he may strengthen you with power through his Spirit in your inner being, so that Christ may dwell in your hearts through faith. And I pray that you, being

*rooted and established in love, may have power, together with all
the saints, to grasp how wide and long and high and deep is the
love of Christ, and to know this love that surpasses knowledge—
that you may be filled to the measure of all the fullness of God*
(Eph. 1:17–19a; 3:16–19).

Set a Goal

As you reflect on these principles and wonderful truths,
what personal need has the Holy Spirit impressed on your
mind and heart? Formulate this need into a specific goal:

_____

_____

_____

Memorize the Following Scripture

*For this reason, since the day we heard about you, we have not
stopped praying for you and asking God to fill you with the
knowledge of his will through all spiritual wisdom and understanding. And we pray this in order that you may live a life worthy of the Lord and may please him in every way: bearing fruit in
every good work, growing in the knowledge of God.*
COLOSSIANS 1:9–10

Growing Together

1. When did you receive the Lord Jesus Christ as your personal Savior? Would you share this experience with us?

2. How do you interpret Romans 12:1–2 in the light of
   what we know about God's desire to have fellowship
   with us day by day?

3. What plan do you have in place—or that you would
   like to put in place—to get to know God better?

4. How can we pray for you specifically?

Chapter 10

Reflecting God's Glory
Read Exodus 34:27–35

No one looks forward to trials and tribulations. They're painful. Yet they play a very important part in God's plan for our lives. In fact, sometimes these painful experiences set the stage for even greater spiritual experiences—as individual Christians, as husbands and wives, and as the church of Jesus Christ.

Moses discovered this on several occasions during his lifetime. He faced his most painful trial and test when Israel rebelled against God and worshiped a golden calf. However, this incredible tribulation set the stage for a profound spiritual experience. It opened up communication between him and God as never before.

Prior to this time, God had been speaking directly to Moses, and Moses directly to God. But Israel's idolatry intensified Moses' fellowship with the Lord, particularly his prayer life. On three successive occasions, Moses prayed earnestly for Israel as he had never prayed before, pleading with the Lord that He would cease being angry with them and withdraw His judgment.

Moses' First Request

"'Turn from your fierce anger; relent and do not bring disaster on your people'" (Exod. 32:12). While Moses was on the mountain with God receiving the Ten Commandments, the children of Israel were down below engaging in flagrant idolatry and immorality. When God told Moses what was happening and what He planned to do about it, he actually begged the Lord not to destroy Israel. Because God loved Moses, He listened to Moses' prayer—even though He was still angry with Israel (32:14). He "changed His mind" and withdrew His hand of judgment. However, He told Moses that He was going to withdraw His presence from Israel. He would send an angel with them but He would not go with them personally for fear He might destroy them in the process (33:2–3). It was this dialogue with the Lord that initiated Moses' second urgent prayer request for Israel.

Moses' Second Request

"'If your Presence does not go with us, do not send us up from here'" (33:15).

Once God promised that He would not destroy Israel completely, Moses then pleaded with the Lord again to change His mind and go with them and not to withdraw His presence. In his first prayer, Moses pleaded: "Please forgive their sin—but if not, then blot me out of the book you have written" (32:32). And in his second prayer, Moses pleaded further: "How will anyone know that you are pleased with me and with your people unless you go with us?" (33:16). In other words, Moses told the Lord that they might as well die right there at the foot of Mount Sinai, for if the Lord did not go with all of them, they would never make it.

Once again, because the Lord loved Moses, He answered his prayer. "My Presence will go with you, and I will give you rest. . . . I will do the very thing you have asked, because I am pleased with you and I know you by name" (33:14, 17). God reinstated His covenant with Israel.

Moses' Third Request

"'Forgive our wickedness and our sin, and take us as your inheritance'" (34:9). Moses' third request for Israel took place when he was once again on top of Mount Sinai. After the Lord had answered his second request, Moses asked to see the Lord's glory. In the midst of a glorious manifestation of the Lord's presence, Moses fell on his face before the Lord and prayed: "'Forgive our wickedness and our sin, and take us as your inheritance'" (34:9). In essence, this is the same request as before—to renew His covenant with Israel and to take them back as His special people and to manifest Himself to the world through them and to bring them into the land as He had promised. Moses needed this reassurance, and the Lord responded with compassion and additional information: "'I am making a covenant with you. Before all your people I will do wonders never before done in any nation in all the world. The people you live among will see how awesome is the work that I, the LORD, will do for you'" (34:10).

Israel, as a nation, was once again back in fellowship with the God they had openly rejected—and the One who had rejected them. Though they and several generations to follow would still suffer the consequences of their sins, God renewed His covenant with Israel (34:6–7, 10). God warned His people, however, that if they ever got involved in idolatry, He would bring divine judgment (34:11–16).

It's obvious that Israel's rebellion impacted Moses. However, rather than running away, he once again turned to God in the midst of this difficult experience. In the process, he personally experienced more of God's presence and power.

Unfortunately, some of us never really pray until we're in trouble. Naturally, this saddens the Lord. But when our prayer life becomes more intense during trials, it's natural and a part of the blessing that comes from experiencing difficult situations. Our whole relationship with God is deepened.

Moses' Greatest Spiritual Experience

After the Lord renewed His covenant with Israel, Moses stayed on top of Mount Sinai for another forty days and forty nights (Exod 34:27–28). God once again gave Moses the Ten Commandments on tablets of stone, replacing the former tablets he had shattered when he discovered the children of Israel worshiping the golden calf (34:1).

During this second period of time, Moses observed more directly God's power and glory. When he came down from the mountain this time, his face literally reflected the glory of God (34:29). This was definitely Moses' greatest spiritual experience. The Lord had revealed His presence as much as possible without literally destroying Moses.

The children of Israel noticed immediately that Moses was different. Though Moses himself was not aware that "his face was radiant" because of his conversation with the Lord, "Aaron and all the Israelites . . . were afraid to come near him" (34:29–30). But once they understood what had happened, all Israel gathered around Moses and listened intently and with open hearts as he shared the message he had received from the Lord (34:31–32).

Moses sensed immediately that the presence of God that was reflected in his face was a significant way to communicate with Israel. Knowing their tendency to forget God, as they had done previously even in the midst of His glorious manifestations, Moses put a veil over his face after he was through speaking the words of God. He did not want them to see the glory of God fade away. When he would go into God's presence, he removed the veil and once again God's glory flooded his soul and was reflected in his face. He would then go out to speak to the people, knowing they would realize that God was speaking through him (34:33, 35).

This was not an ego trip for Moses. It was a sincere strategy to help the children of Israel respond to the Lord. After all, he had offered his own life if God did not redeem Israel. He had prayed and pleaded with God not to destroy them, to continue to be present with them, and to restore His covenant. God answered Moses' prayers, and the glory that was reflected in his face was an unexpected blessing to help him communicate with a group of people that God Himself called "stiff-necked" and rebellious.

A More Glorious Covenant

The apostle Paul mentioned Moses' second forty-day experience on Mount Sinai in his second letter to the Corinthians (2 Cor. 3:1–18). In the overall passage, Paul was defending his apostleship. He stated that the greatest proof of his divine appointment in ministry was the Corinthians themselves. Other teachers were carrying around actual letters of commendation and recommendation. However, Paul told the Corinthians that *they* were his "letter"—a letter "known and read by everybody." More specifically, he said: "You show that you are a letter from Christ, the result of our ministry, written not with ink but with the Spirit of the living God, not on tablets of stone but on tablets of human hearts" (2 Cor. 3:3).

This is a powerful and wonderful truth. Paul was teaching that a New Testament body of Christians should reflect God's glory, just as Moses reflected God's glory when he received the Ten Commandments—and even more so. Paul demonstrated this truth with a series of contrasts between the old and the new covenants (2 Cor. 3:7–9, 11; emphasis added) (see p.136).

Paul culminated this great section of Scripture with a challenge to all Christians:

"And we, who with unveiled faces all reflect the Lord's glory, are being transformed into his likeness with ever-increasing glory, which comes from the Lord, who is the Spirit" (3:18).

What does Paul mean? First, no Christian need ever veil his face like Moses. The light of Jesus Christ should shine

Old Covenant	New Covenant
*Now if the ministry that brought death, which was engraved in letters on stone, came with **glory**, so that the Israelites could not look steadily at the face of Moses because of its **glory**, fading though it was,*	*will not the ministry of the Spirit be even **more glorious**?* (vv. 7–8)
*If the ministry that condemns men is **glorious**,*	*how much **more glorious** is the ministry that brings righteousness!* (v. 9)
*And if what was fading away came with **glory**,*	*How much **greater is the glory** of that which lasts!* (v. 11)

through our lives every moment of every day. His glory need never fade. The opposite should be true. The more we develop our relationship with Christ, the more we should reflect Christ's glory. The more we study the Scriptures, the more His image should be reflected. And the more we allow the Word of God and the Spirit of God to change our lives, the more we will be transformed into the men and women God wants us to become!

A second thing Paul is stating to the Corinthians—and to us—is that the Lord does not expect individual Christians to reflect His glory by themselves. As a body of believers, we are to reflect the image of Christ. In the Old Testament, God manifested His glory through individuals—men like Moses. But in the New Testament, God's basic plan is that His functioning church reflect His glory. In fact, it is only as the body of Christ functions as God intended that we can reflect certain aspects of Christ's life, such as the unity Jesus had with the Father. This is what Jesus prayed for prior to His death on the cross. As you read this portion of Christ's prayer, note how unity among Christians reflects the *incarnation* as well as the *glory* of God:

"'My prayer is not for them alone. I pray also for those who will believe in me through their message, that all of them may be one, Father, just as you are in me and I am in you. May they also be in us so that the world may believe that you have sent me. I have given them *the glory that you gave me*, that they may be one as we are one: I in them and you in me. May they be brought to complete unity to let the world know that you sent me and have loved them even as you have loved me'" (John 17:20–23).

Another example relates to Paul's teaching regarding the fruit of the Spirit. Frequently, we apply this verse to individuals. However, Paul was speaking to local bodies of believers in his Galatian letter. Together, we are to reflect "love, joy, peace, patience, kindness, goodness, faithfulness, gentleness and self-control" (Gal. 5:22). Most of these qualities are relational in nature. They cannot be reflected effectively by individual Christians. For example, the only way people can see Christ's love in my life is to see me loving someone else. Though they may be able to see "joy" in me personally, the greatest reflection of joy is when I join my heart in praise and adoration to God with other believers. Other qualities that are definitely corporate are "patience," "kindness," and "gentleness"—which must be demonstrated toward *one another*.

In essence, Paul is teaching that as a local body of Christians grows and matures in Christ, that corporate entity will increasingly reflect the glory of Jesus Christ—becoming more and more like Him. When we become one as Christ is one with the Father, His life is once again "fleshed out" and the world can see His glory!

Becoming God's Man Today

Principles To Live By

There are at least three powerful principles that relate to Moses' experience:

Principle 1. When we face trials, we should always attempt to view these experiences as opportunities to grow in our relationship with God.

James elaborates on this principle: "Consider it pure joy, my brothers, whenever you face trials of many kinds, because you know that the testing of your faith develops perseverance. Perseverance must finish its work so that you may be mature and complete, not lacking anything" (James 1:2–4).

Pure joy, you say! How can I enjoy trials? To "enjoy" something and to experience "pure joy" are two different dimensions in our human experience. Joy per se indicates positive feelings. "Pure joy" involves a sense of peace in the midst of emotional pain. It's supernatural! It cannot be explained completely in human terms.

Furthermore, James said it is something we should "consider." He didn't say, "Experience pure joy" when you're going through various trials. Rather, if our attitude is right, we are able to see beyond the pain and with the eye of faith see the way this particular difficulty will draw us close to God and enable us to reflect His glory and character to others.

If it were not for the problems and difficulties in our lives, we would tend to rely on our own efforts and abilities. Trials and tests can draw us closer to God and produce great spiritual experiences—experiences we might never have had were it not for the difficulties of life. This is why Paul also wrote that we should "rejoice in our sufferings, because we know that suffering produces perseverance; perseverance character; and character, hope. And hope does not disappoint us, because God has poured out his love into our hearts by the Holy Spirit, whom he has given us" (Rom. 5:3–5).

Principle 2. When we face trials, we must remember that God has designed prayer as a divine resource to help us through these trials.

This was Moses' secret. He took his burdens to the Lord. He asked God for help. He pleaded with the Lord. This is why James also follows his exhortation regarding trials with a reference to prayer: "If any of you lacks wisdom, he should ask God, who gives generously to all without finding fault, and it will be given to him" (James 1:5).

Paul also encouraged the Philippians—and us—to pray when we face difficult problems: "Do not be anxious about anything, but in everything, by prayer and petition, with thanksgiving, present your requests to God. And the peace of God, which transcends all understanding, will guard your hearts and your minds in Christ Jesus" (Phil. 4:6–7).

Again, don't misunderstand. We cannot avoid anxiety when we face trials. However, we can allow that anxiety to drive us to the Lord in prayer. This is what happened to Moses. He was terribly anxious, but he poured it all out to God—his frustration, his fears, his confusion. In the midst of this process, he began to experience God's peace! This is what God has also designed for all of us when we face painful periods in our lives.

Principle 3. God wants to use trials in our own lives to be able to reflect His glory to others.

Painful experiences drive us to our knees to seek God's strength. It's in moments like this we learn to know more about God and experience His divine presence. In turn, this gives us opportunities to share God's glory with others.

Some of the most mature Christians—and churches—I know are those who have endured trials victoriously. To quote

Peter, their "faith" is "of greater worth than gold" (1 Pet. 1:7). Furthermore, they are people who can minister to others effectively when they are going through the same trials. They can identify with the apostle Paul who wrote to the Corinthians: "Praise be to the God and Father of our Lord Jesus Christ, the Father of compassion and the God of all comfort, who comforts us in all our troubles, so that we can comfort those in any trouble with the comfort we ourselves have received from God" (2 Cor. 1:3–4).

Personalizing These Principles

The following questions will help you to apply these principles when you face various trials and tribulations:

1. When you face a trial, do you attempt to see a divine purpose that can come out of this difficulty, or do you become so trapped in the problem that you can't see beyond the immediate situation?

2. When you face various trials, do you go to the Lord, not simply asking for help, but pouring out all your emotional pain and hurts? Are you reverently honest with God?

3. When you face various trials, do you try to see how God can use this painful experience to help you ultimately reflect His glory to others? Do you attempt to see how God can use this experience to help someone else who is going through a similar difficulty?

Set a Goal

What one particular goal do you need to set based on this study:

_____

_____

_____

_____

Memorize the Following Scripture

And we know that in all things God works for the good of those who love him, who have been called according to his purpose.
ROMANS 8:28.

Growing Together

1. Why is it difficult to see God's purpose in the midst of a difficult trial?

2. How has God used pain and suffering in your life to draw you closer to Himself? How have you seen this in the lives of others?

3. How has God enriched your prayer life because of difficult circumstances?

4. How have you been helped by other Christians who can identify with your own painful experiences?

5. How can we pray for you specifically?

Chapter 11

From Elation to Depression
Read Numbers 10:33–11:33

*C*an a Christian ever become so depressed he wants to give up—to quit? We feel great one day—and just a short time later, we find ourselves in a pit of despair. Is it possible to move quickly from having a strong faith in God to having virtually no faith at all? Can we have an overwhelming sense of God's presence and power and then become so depressed we feel God has forsaken us and we literally want to die?

Moses had all of these thoughts and feelings—just three days after he led Israel to break camp at Mount Sinai. He went from "the top of the mountain" where he communicated with God "face to face" as a friend communicates with his friend to a state of utter desperation! Moses lost total perspective and cried out to God, "If this is how you are going to treat me, put me to death right now" (Num. 11:15a).

Gaining Perspective

Israel had camped at Sinai for one year. A lot had happened—both to Israel and to their leader, Moses. It was here the children of Israel committed their greatest sin—worshiping a golden calf. But it was also here that Moses passed his greatest test—his relentless intercession for Israel.

Israel also received God's law at Mount Sinai—not only the moral law as embodied in the Ten Commandments, but the laws of God which were to govern their civil and religious life. In fact, all twenty-seven chapters of Leviticus and the first nine chapters of Numbers record God's Word to Israel through Moses. The statement "Then the LORD spoke to Moses, saying" (or a similar one) appears nearly sixty times.

It was at Sinai that Moses experienced communion with God that can only be compared to the fellowship Adam had with the Lord in the Garden of Eden prior to his disobedience. Moses talked with God face to face—as friend with friend. The Lord revealed His glory through Moses' countenance, and the children of Israel responded with openness and willing obedience.

But the day finally came for Israel to move on, to leave Sinai and travel toward Canaan (Num. 10:11–13). The cloud that hovered over the Tabernacle suddenly began to move. Since God had "changed His mind" and decided to maintain a special presence with Israel, they all knew it was time to break camp and follow the Lord (Exod. 40:34–38).

Ungrateful Contention

Moses was very optimistic and enthusiastic when they broke camp, no doubt because of his personal communion with the Lord over the past twelve months and Israel's positive response to the Word of God. He had great faith in the Lord, which is evident in his prayer regarding the Ark of God which was now an important part of their place of worship in the Tabernacle. We read that "whenever the Ark set out, Moses said, 'Rise up, O LORD! May our enemies be scattered; may your foes flee before you.' Whenever it came to rest, he said, 'Return, O LORD, to the countless thousands of Israel'" (Num. 10:35–36).

Moses was greatly encouraged that God had promised not to withdraw His presence. But then it happened! In fact, the timing was ironic. Just three days after leaving Sinai

(Num. 10:33), Israel began to complain (Num. 11:1), just as they had done three days after they had sung Moses' song of victory following their marvelous deliverance from the Egyptians when they crossed the Red Sea (Exod. 15:22–24). For Moses, it was like tearing open an old wound that had been healed over.

To make matters worse, Israel had far less to complain about than previously. Furthermore, they had a much greater knowledge of God's Word and will for their lives. When they first complained at Marah, they had no water to drink, but now there was no lack. At Marah, God had not spoken directly to Israel, but this time they complained in the full light of God's visual and verbal revelation which had come thundering from Sinai.

Instantly, the Lord demonstrated His displeasure toward Israel. Once again He became angry and sent fire that "consumed some of the outskirts of the camp" (Num. 11:1).

Obviously, this was a serious warning—but also an act of grace. God was keeping His promise to Moses not to suddenly destroy the children of Israel, to wipe them off the face of the earth as He had warned Moses that He might do if He continued to be among them on their journey to Canaan (Exod. 33:3).

Moses responded to this initial crisis well. He quickly interceded for Israel, and God listened and "the fire died down" (Num. 11:2). But he was not emotionally prepared for the next event. Many of the sons of Israel ignored God's gracious warning and began to complain. "'If only we had meat to eat!'" they whined. "'We remember the fish we ate in Egypt at no cost—also the cucumbers, melons, leeks, onions and garlic. . . . We never see anything but this manna!'" (11:4–6).

It was not a matter of having no food! Rather, they wanted better food! They were not satisfied with God's generous provision of manna, His glorious presence at Sinai and in the Tabernacle, and His gracious promise that He would eventually bring them to the land of Canaan—to a land of plenty that would make Egypt's vegetables and fruit seem as nothing. What happened is obvious! Many of these people had already forgotten God's love and grace and what He had done for them—just three days after their incredible year at Mount Sinai.

Intense Depression

Moses' joy suddenly turned to sadness and deep depression. At that moment he probably feared that God was going to forsake Israel and leave them in his hands! He felt the weight of the whole problem resting squarely on his shoulders.

The Scriptures state that "Moses was troubled" (11:10). In fact he was *deeply* troubled! He was ready to give up, to quit. What Moses said to the Lord reflects a man who was terribly distressed and anxious about his ability to cope with the demands that he believed God was about to put on him.

He Lost Sight of God's Promises

Moses thought God had forsaken him. He took God's judgment on Israel very personally. Listen to his prayer: "'Why have you brought this trouble on your servant? What have I done to displease you that you put the burden of all these people on me? Did I conceive all these people? Did I give them birth?'" (11:11–12a).

What Moses said next gives us insight as to what he feared God was going to do. Needless to say, he was both disgusted with Israel's immaturity and terribly paranoid regarding what might happen: "'Why do you tell me to carry them in my arms, as a nurse carries an infant, to the land you promised on oath to their forefathers?'" (11:12b).

Moses was afraid God might leave him with the total responsibility of leading Israel into the promised land. He knew only too well how frustrated and angry the Lord became with Israel because of their sins. It's easy to understand that in his humanness he assumed that God was forsaking His people—that he alone would have to bear the burden. After all, this is what God had already threatened to do (Exod. 33:3, 14–16).

Moses—like most of us in a crisis situation—forgot God's promises both to himself and to Israel. There were no "ands," no "ifs," and no "buts" about their initial possession of the land. God was going to go with them. He had definitely renewed His covenant with Israel (Exod. 34:10). He was not going to start over with Moses and his family. But even though God had made a promise, somehow in the midst of a dark moment, Moses forgot it. Sound familiar?

He Lost Sight of God's Power

"'Where can I get meat for all these people?'" Moses asked the Lord (Num. 11:13). Even after God had told Moses He would provide, he still had difficulty believing. "'Here I am among six hundred thousand men on foot,'" Moses responded to the Lord. "'And you say "I will give them meat to eat for a whole month!"'" (11:21).

At this point God had to remind Moses of his strong and mighty arm. "'Is the LORD's arm too short?'" the Lord asked. "'You will now see whether or not what I say will come true for you'" (11:23).

What a contrast! Could this be the same Moses that penned the great song of victory following the Red Sea experience? Could this be the Moses who cried out, "'Your right hand, O LORD, was majestic in power. Your right hand, O LORD, shattered the enemy'" (Exod. 15:6).

To be sure, this was the same man—but his hopes for Israel had been dashed! He was in a state of despair. To be fair, Moses was not only doubting God's power to provide meat for the people, but he was also doubting that Israel would ever be satisfied. This is why he also asked the Lord, "'Would they have enough if flocks and herds were slaughtered for them? *Would they have enough if all the fish in the sea were caught for them?'"* (Num. 11:22).

This is total disillusionment! Moses didn't trust God, and he didn't trust the people. He had lost hope! He wanted out. He felt trapped between the God he had tried to serve and the people he had been willing to die for. In this state of weariness and depression, he lost sight of what God had already done for Israel—on many occasions—and he felt betrayed by the people he had loved and served so faithfully.

Considering all of the circumstances, Moses' response is predictable. Though most of us will never face the same challenges as Moses, we experience similar emotions when we're tired, distraught, and facing unusual pressures. We, too, quickly lose sight of God's power.

He Lost Perspective of God's Overall Plan

In desperation, Moses cried out to the Lord, "'I cannot carry all of these people by myself; the burden is too heavy for me'" (11:14).

Ever since God called to Moses from the burning bush, He had promised His servant that He would be with him and help carry out this great task of leading the children of Israel out of Egypt and into the promised land. Even when He threatened to withdraw His presence from Israel, He still promised that He would be with Moses and send an angel with them as they continued the journey (Exod. 33:2, 14). But in the midst of this crisis, Moses' memory faded. What he knew in both his head and his heart suddenly seemed to be lost in a mass of negative emotions and feelings that were so overwhelming that he wanted God to take his life. If the Lord were going to forsake him, Moses wanted to end it right then and there! "'If this is how you are going to treat me,'" he cried out to the Lord, "'put me to death right now . . . do not let me face my own ruin'" (Num. 11:15).

Moses was telling God that if he had to lead Israel by himself, he would die anyway. He wouldn't be able to hold up under the pressure. He begged the Lord to have mercy on him and to get it over with! Sudden death would be much better than wasting away in the midst of his agony and despair.

The most encouraging aspect of this story is that God understood Moses' feelings of resentment and despair. After all, the Lord Himself was so angry with Israel that He wanted to destroy them. Why wouldn't God understand Moses—a mere human being—who was experiencing some of the same feelings that God had felt.

This is not the last time that one of God's choice servants became depressed. Centuries later, Elijah would experience the same emotions. After his incredible victory over the prophets of Baal, Elijah fled into the wilderness, sat down under a tree, and asked God to take his life (1 Kings 19:4).

God responded to Elijah with great compassion. He understood his total exhaustion. He allowed him to sleep and eat. Elijah then traveled on, refreshed and strengthened (1 Kings 19:8). The Lord met Elijah's need—and He did the same for Moses.

Positive Solutions

A Support Team

God instituted a plan that was similar to the one Jethro had proposed at Mount Sinai (Exod. 18:17–26). He instructed Moses to select seventy men from the elders of Israel that he knew personally and who were already doing a good job as leaders. They were to assemble around the Tabernacle where they could see the Lord descend in the cloud and hear Him speak to Moses. The Lord would then come upon these men with His Spirit, empowering them to assist Moses. Even so, Moses questioned God's power and poured out his negative feelings regarding Israel's insatiable appetite for the "good things in life" (Num. 11:21–22). But the Lord immediately reassured Moses that he could and would solve the problem (11:23).

Did Moses doubt at this moment because the first part of God's solution involved the men of Israel? Probably. He had even lost faith in his most faithful leaders. Again, this is understandable. Once again, God could identify with Moses' feelings. When Israel had camped at the foot of Mount Sinai, He too had given up on these very same men. Furthermore, these were the men for whom Moses had interceded when God wanted to "destroy them" (Exod. 32:10).

In spite of Moses' lack of faith, he responded to God's instructions. Like the man who brought his demon-possessed son to Jesus, he was saying, "'I do believe; help me overcome my unbelief'" (Mark 9:24). The Lord honored what faith Moses had. He knew His servant needed encouragement and help and that he could not carry out this task all by himself. Consequently, the Lord anointed seventy other men who could help Moses bear the burden of his leadership position. Furthermore, He gave these men the same spiritual power that He had given to Moses: "Then the LORD came down in the cloud and spoke with him, and he took the Spirit that was on him and put the Spirit on the seventy elders" (Num. 11:25).

Divine Judgment

The second aspect of God's plan to help Moses involved His judgment on Israel. It was purely a divine solution. The people asked for meat, and God gave them what they asked. He caused a wind to drive "quail in from the sea." When this huge flock of birds arrived where Israel was camped, they floundered and fell to the earth. In some places they were stacked up three feet deep. The people rushed out to gather up the quail. But we read that "while the meat was still between their teeth and before it could be consumed, the anger of the LORD burned against the people and he struck them with a severe plague" (11:33). All the people that had complained died. God brought judgment upon them because of their greed and ungrateful attitudes. He removed the grumblers from the camp of Israel so Moses would never have to contend with them again.

Becoming God's Man Today

Principles to Live By

There are some very practical lessons we can learn from Moses' bout with depression. Though the circumstances were entirely different than ours will ever be, the spiritual and emotional dynamics are often the same for all of us. We can experience some of the same feelings as Moses in our contemporary society, even though our problems are focused in our marriages, our churches, and in our places of business.

Principle 1. In the midst of intense pressure and complex problems, we tend to forget God's promises and power— and we lose perspective on His plan for our lives.

No matter how close we've been to God in the past, or how many times He has answered our prayers, and no matter how clear our perspective and exciting our lives, we can hit a low point that literally "wipes us out." In fact, during times of unusual stress it is not uncommon to think the thoughts that Moses and Elijah thought—that we would "rather be dead."

Furthermore, depression can hit quickly, just as it did with Moses and Elijah. This is particularly true when we've been through a series of difficult circumstances that tend to lower our spiritual, emotional, and physical resistances. This is when we're most vulnerable. If it happened to some of God's greatest servants, don't be surprised if it happens to you. And when it does, it will affect your ability to think, feel, and act properly.

Principle 2. God understands the difficult periods in our lives and desires that we share our feelings with Him.

God knows our plight, our predicaments, our feelings of totally being "out of it." He understood Moses and Elijah, and He understands us. He knows that we're simply human beings. He knows all about our weaknesses. He is well aware that we sometimes get terribly tired and horribly frustrated and sometimes intensely fearful and angry. Furthermore, he welcomes us to lay our hearts bare before Him. He will not judge us. If we feel like dying, we can tell Him so—and He understands!

Recently, I was counseling a young man who is going through a terrible period of emotional pain. *Unlike Moses,* he had created his own mess. But even then he told how he had poured out his feelings of frustration to God, venting his anger and emotional turmoil. He even went so far as to ask God to strike him dead. He then fell exhausted on the ground, weeping uncontrollably.

The rest of the story reflects God's unconditional love. While lying there in a spiritually and emotionally broken condition, this young man suddenly felt God's love overwhelming him. It was as if the Lord gently put His arms around him and told him He really cared, that He really understood his feelings. It was then my friend sensed that God was telling him that He wanted to help him but He couldn't—not until this young man was willing to give up the secret sins in his life. Even in this case, when one of His children deliberately walked out of the will of God, the Lord demonstrated compassion and concern.

Principle 3. We should seek God's solutions to our depression.

If we get depressed because of sin in our lives—like the young man I just told you about—we need to deal with that sin. There is no other solution. We need to confess it to God, ask forgiveness from others if we have wronged them, and then, with God's help, continue to do the will of God (1 John 1:9).

However, not all depression is caused by specific sin in our own lives. Elijah had exerted so much energy and experienced so much stress doing God's work that he was on the verge of a nervous breakdown.

False guilt. Some of us get depressed because we feel guilty about things we shouldn't feel guilty about. We have not violated the will of God but false, man-made standards. However, whether it is true guilt or false guilt, it still causes depression. If we're experiencing false guilt, we need to tune our consciences to the Word of God.

I faced this problem in my own life as a young man. I had been reared in a very exclusive and legalistic religious community. Much of what I had been taught regarding "spirituality" was based on tradition not Scripture. When I understood that my guilt was often "false guilt," I was able to be freed from this emotional and spiritual bondage. However, it took time and a very understanding friend who helped me "dig out of the pit" that often caused depression in my life.

Physical problems. Some Christians get depressed as a result of hormonal imbalances. If you cannot isolate a particular cause of depression, immediately get a physical examination from a competent medical doctor. In recent years there have been incredible breakthroughs in treating depression that has physical rather than mental or spiritual causes. As a pastor, I have seen people's lives totally transformed when glandular imbalances have been restored with proper medications. Furthermore, if there were other stresses that had led to this condition, they were then able to deal with the root cause of their problems.

Environmental barriers. Some Christians get depressed because of their environment. For example, I've seen young mothers get terribly depressed because they've been cooped up day after day in their homes with their young children. Predictably, at times they have feelings of anger and have no way to express these feelings legitimately. If they continue in this situation without a break, depression is inevitable. The only solution is for them to be able to get away periodically, to change their environment, and to be freed up from their demanding routines.

As husbands we need to be very sensitive to our wives. Remember, too, when a young Christian mother gets angry, she often feels guilty—and guilt only compounds her problem. At this moment she needs an understanding listener who can reassure her that what she's feeling is normal. Sadly, these conditions can lead to abuse—which is a tragedy for both parents and children.

Demanding work. Some people get depressed because of the demands in their own work. They often face competition that is at times unfair, which in turn generates angry feelings. And when they succeed in "crowding someone else out," they feel guilty, particularly if they're sensitive to others' needs. The twentieth-century "rat-race" culture can play havoc with our emotions. Men, too, need understanding wives, as well as faithful male friends who can help bear their burdens.

Irresponsibility. Some of us get depressed because we don't use common sense. We overwork, we plan poorly, we overextend ourselves, and we set our goals too high. Though the Lord understands the dilemmas we create for ourselves, we must take action to correct these problems.

Self-condemnation. Remember, too, that depression with its accompanying guilt gets worse when we condemn ourselves. If our depression is caused by sin, we can settle that with God—today! His solution is to accept the forgiveness that we have in Jesus Christ because of His shed blood on the cross (1 John 1:9). However, if our depression is brought on by other causes, we must realize that God understands. We must not condemn ourselves—that only makes the problem worse. But we must also remember that we are responsible—with God's help—to find the solution to our problems and to act on that solution.[1]

Personalizing These Principles

If we're depressed and have lost perspective on God's promises and His power, we must not add to our problem by allowing guilt to drive us deeper into a "slough of despond." Remember that God understands your problem and wants to help you find a solution. Then seek help from a trusted friend or counselor. Though you should certainly feel free to share your thoughts and feelings with the Lord, remember He has designed the body of Christ to be a healing organism. We need to share our problems and concerns with other Christians who can help us.

Be cautious, however. Some well-meaning Christians will attempt to "spiritualize" all emotional problems. When depression has another cause, this can only compound the problem. If this happens, talk to someone who is more competent and knowledgeable in dealing with this kind of human difficulty. Make sure, however, that whomever you consult has a total perspective that takes into consideration the spiritual dimensions of our lives as well as the emotional and physical.

Set a Goal

Reread the section in this chapter entitled "Principles to Live By." Ask the Holy Spirit to encourage you and to help you discover what may be causing depression in your own life or in the life of someone who is close to you. Then set a specific goal:

_____

_____

_____

_____

Memorize the Following Scripture

Is any one of you sick? He should call the elders of the church to pray over him and anoint him with oil in the name of the Lord. And the prayer offered in faith will make the sick person well; the Lord will raise him up. If he has sinned, he will be forgiven. Therefore confess your sins to each other and pray for each other so that you may be healed. The prayer of a righteous man is powerful and effective.

JAMES 5:14–16

Growing Together

1. Why is it so easy to lose perspective on God's promises and power when we're depressed?

2. Would you feel free to share what has caused depression in your own life and how you solved the problem?

3. Why is it so important to discover what is the root cause of depression—understanding that not all depression is a direct result of deliberate sin in our lives?

4. How can we pray for you specifically?

Chapter 12

The Pain of Unjust Criticism
Read Num. 12:1–16; 16:1–15

*P*ersonal criticism that is *justified* is one thing. Even when we deserve it, it's always painful. But criticism that is *unjust* hurts even more—especially if it comes from someone we've loved and trusted—those who should be the most understanding. What makes this kind of criticism even more excruciating is their questioning our motives, calling us dishonest, or accusing us of pride when in reality none of these accusations are true. Believe it or not, after all Moses went through to lead God's people out of Egypt, he faced this kind of unjust criticism.

Gaining Perspective

Moses had already fought a lot of personal battles with Israel—their complaining, their idolatry, and their immorality. But no one had yet attacked him personally, questioning his motives and accusing him of pride and self exaltation, and actually blaming him for the judgment that God brought on Israel.

But it happened! As you read and study the life of this great leader, you really wonder how much stress and turmoil one man can take. Moses of course would have given up long before these false accusations came his way if had he faced these struggles all alone. But God had promised him that He would never leave him—and He never did. In fact, the moment the Lord heard these unjust criticisms, He moved into action quickly and did something about it. In view of all that Moses had done for Israel—actually pleading for their lives—the Lord did not allow him to face this painful experience by himself.

There's an interesting sequence in the biblical account. First, Moses was criticized by his own brother and sister. Second, he was blind-sided by his own leaders, men he had chosen and trusted implicitly. Third, he was accused falsely by the whole congregation.

Unjust Criticism from His Own Family

Moses must have been crushed when his own sister and brother, Miriam and Aaron, accused him of pride—of thinking that he had a more important leadership position than they had.

A Powerful Emotion

Jealousy often causes people to strike out at others, and that's what motivated Miriam and Aaron. At first, they "smoke-screened" their real motives. They criticized their brother for marrying a Cushite woman—someone who was not "one of them" (Num. 12:1). In essence, they were accusing Moses of being inconsistent and violating God's law to never marry an idolater (Exod. 34:16).

Why bring this issue up now? Moses had married Zipporah, a Midianite, years before, when he had fled from Egypt after trying to take matters into his own hands. He was not even aware of God's laws that he would later receive from God on the top of Mount Sinai. In fact, when God spoke to him from the burning bush, he was just getting to know the God of Abraham, Isaac, and Jacob. He had been exposed to Egyptian paganism for forty years and to the Midianite religion for another forty years.

Of all people, Miriam and Aaron should have understood Moses' situation. It's clear they were simply looking for a reason to "put Moses down" so they could "build themselves up." They were trying to demonstrate to the people in Israel that they—along with Moses—were just as capable of telling others what was right and what was wrong. Consequently, the more they talked, the more they revealed the *real* reason they were attacking Moses: "'Has the Lord spoken only through Moses?' they asked. 'Hasn't He also spoken through us?'" (Num. 12:2). Their motivation was "green-eyed" jealousy!

If Miriam and Aaron had a sincere concern about Moses' past life and his present spiritual condition, they would have approached him privately. However, this would not have served their purpose. They were really concerned about themselves. They wanted others in Israel to know that they, too, were capable of leading Israel. They wanted more of the spotlight. This is why they made their accusation public—using Moses' marriage to a Cushite as a basis for parading their "own wisdom." They were trying to prove that they too had special favor with God.

A Forgiving Spirit

Even if we had no previous knowledge of Moses' life, simply watching the way he responded to this false criticism reveals who was right and who was wrong. Though it is not always inappropriate to defend ourselves against false criticism, Moses did not defend himself in this situation. Because of his humility and his deep love for his brother and sister, he did not try to justify himself or to correct them. Even if he had been tempted to lash out, he restrained himself and waited for the truth to come to light. Obviously he was trying to protect Miriam and Aaron, even though they were trying to embarrass him before all Israel.

Why this gracious approach? For one thing, Moses certainly never forgot that it was Miriam who had been such an important part of God's plan in saving him from a watery grave when he was just a baby (Exod 2:4–8). It was also Miriam who led the women of Israel in singing the song of praise that Moses wrote after they had crossed the Red Sea (15:20–21). He would never have forgotten that glorious scene. And as far as we know, Miriam had been loyal to Moses all during her journey thus far. Whatever his reason, Moses did not respond harshly to either Miriam or Aaron. In this sense, he "turned the other cheek" (Matt. 5:39).

However, God was definitely "listening in" and stepped into the scene immediately. He honored Moses' humility and his willingness to bear this false accusation without defending himself. First, God let Miriam and Aaron know that they were seriously "out of order." They were *not* on the same level as Moses. Even though Miriam was a prophetess and Aaron a high priest, God only spoke to them through visions and dreams. But not so with Moses! "'With him,'" God said, "'I speak face to face, clearly and not in riddles; he sees the form of the LORD'" (Num. 12:8). This is why the Holy Spirit added the final addendum to Moses' account of Israel's history and said, "No prophet has risen in Israel like Moses, *whom the LORD knew face to face*" (Deut. 34:10).

God was angry with Miriam and Aaron—even though Moses was not. "'Why then were you not afraid to speak against my servant Moses?'" He asked them very directly (Num. 12:8b–9). Because Miriam had evidently instigated this plot against Moses, the Lord struck her with leprosy (12:9–10).

Following Rather than Leading

Aaron had once again demonstrated a serious weakness in his own personality. He was more of a follower than a leader. At Sinai, he had succumbed to Israel's pleas to mold a golden calf and then rationalized his behavior when he was confronted with his sin (Exod. 32:24). This time he followed Miriam in criticizing Moses. He was not only a weak leader, but also lacked discernment.

However, Aaron's reaction to God's judgment on his sister also reveals a tender heart. Combined with his weakness was a strength. He confessed his sin immediately (Num.12:11) and expressed deep concern for his sister (12:12). Perhaps he was motivated by guilt and fear—that he, too, might be struck with the same affliction. However, we also see true repentance and deep compassion. God honored both his remorse and his prayer for his sister.

Overcoming Evil with Good

Moses' reaction to all of this is mind-boggling. He held no grudges! Furthermore, he did not use this as an opportunity to demonstrate to Israel the "wrongness" of their behavior and the "rightness" of his. If he had been an opportunist, looking for a chance to vindicate himself, here it was! Miriam was leprous—white "like snow" (12:10), and Aaron was begging for mercy (12:11). What a unique moment for Moses to defend himself—and in front of all Israel!

But Moses used this opportunity to pray for his sister. "'O God, please heal her!'" he cried out to God (12:13). Once again, God responded to Moses' prayer, but only after allowing Miriam to remain in her condition for seven days outside the camp. Healing her immediately would not have made the point God wanted to make in the presence of all Israel. For a whole week they remained camped in that place while they waited for Miriam to heal. God had both defended Moses' reputation and at the same time taught Israel a very important lesson—not to attack his servant Moses with unjust criticisms and false accusations.

Unjust Criticism from His Fellow Leaders

Not surprising, the leaders in Israel quickly forgot this lesson. Not only did they fail to remember what had happened to Miriam, they forgot the judgment that fell on them because they had failed to go into the promised land as God had instructed (13:1–14:45). They would have to wander in the wilderness for forty years until the older generation died. Only those under twenty years of age would be allowed to enter into the promised land (14:26–35). Furthermore, the ten spies who had disobeyed God and demoralized their fellow Israelites all died from a terrible plague (14:36–38). And when the rest of the children of Israel had found out about the "forty-year sentence," they had tried to compensate for their horrible mistake by going up to take the land in their own strength, only to suffer terrible defeat at the hands of the Canaanites and Amalekites (14:45).

After all of these warnings and judgments, a group of leaders still had the gall to falsely accuse Moses. This time Korah, a descendant of Levi and one of Moses' trusted leaders, was the instigator. He influenced three other leaders—Dathan, Abiram, and On—to rebel (16:1). They in turn influenced 250 other "men of renown," and convinced them to join in a conspiracy against Moses (16:2).

Once these men formulated their plan, they all "came as a group to oppose Moses and Aaron and said to them, 'You have gone too far! The whole community is holy, every one of them, and the LORD is with them. Why then do you set yourselves above the LORD's assembly?'" (16:3). When Moses heard this accusation he was dumbfounded—so much so that "he fell facedown" (16:4).

How could this be? He and Aaron had simply followed the instructions of the Lord—not their own desires. Furthermore, if the Lord had allowed Moses to have his own way, he would have given up his leadership role a long time ago. Think of the many times he had pleaded for the lives of the Israelites—even wanting to die if God did not withhold His hand of judgment. Think how traumatic it was for Moses to see leaders he had chosen, trusted, and sacrificed for twist the truth because of their jealousy and desire for positions of power. Why hadn't they remembered what had happened to his sister Miriam and to his brother Aaron when they had falsely accused him—and for a similar reason?

Again, Moses' reactions are truly amazing! He immediately turned the problem over to the Lord who showed him what to do. Moses went directly to Korah, the perpetrator, who was a Levite with responsibilities to serve in the tabernacle (16:5–10). Moses confronted him "and all of his followers" (16:5), accusing them of having selfish motives. They weren't satisfied with their ministry positions in Israel. They also wanted to take over the priesthood (16:10).

Because these men wouldn't listen to Moses' warnings, God's solution was dramatic—and awesome. After giving them numerous opportunities to repent and turn from their evil ways, the Lord opened up the earth and it swallowed Korah, Dathan, and Abiram and their entire families (16:11–34). Furthermore, the 250 men who had joined in this conspiracy were also destroyed by fire that came forth from the Lord while they were trying to demonstrate to everyone that they were just as holy as Moses and Aaron (16:35).

Once again, God had defended Moses. This time Aaron was on the receiving end of this false criticism, experiencing a dose of his own medicine. But God in His mercy also defended him because of his repentance and his desire to serve as a faithful high priest in Israel.

Unjust Criticism from All Israel

In spite of this incredible visual demonstration of God's judgment on the leaders of Israel, "the whole Israelite community grumbled against Moses and Aaron." They actually accused them of having "killed the LORD's people" (16:41).

Again, how could this be? These people had just seen what had happened. However, their thinking was so distorted that they blamed Moses and Aaron. At this point God's anger was so stirred up against Israel that He was once again ready to destroy them all (16:42–45). But once again, Moses—man of God that he was—began to intercede for the very ones who had falsely accused him. Even though judgment fell in the form of a severe plague and wiped out 14,700 of the people, the majority were saved because Moses and Aaron made atonement for Israel's sin, burning incense before the Lord (16:46–50).

A Picture of Christ's Suffering

The author of the book of Hebrews gives us an unusual insight into Moses' life and how the sacrifices he made for Israel beautifully describe what Jesus Christ has done for the whole world: "He regarded disgrace *for the sake of Christ* as of greater value than the treasures of Egypt, because he was looking ahead to his reward" (Heb. 11:26).

Moses suffered periods of great pain after he chose to give up his position in Egypt. However, what we've just seen in this chapter correlates in a very unique way with what happened to Jesus Christ when He gave up the glories of heaven to dwell among us.

First, Jesus Christ, like Moses, *was rejected by members of his own family.* Even his own brothers did not accept Him as the promised Messiah (John 7:5).

Second, Jesus Christ, like Moses, *was rejected by the leadership of Israel.* The Pharisees and Sadducees and other religious leaders were his greatest enemies. They were threatened by his claims—and his presence. And their primary motivation was jealousy. (John 11:48, 53).

Third, Jesus Christ, like Moses, *was rejected by all Israel.* John writes that: "He came to that which was his own [the nation Israel], but his own did not receive Him" (John 1:11).

The children of Israel as a nation rejected Jesus Christ. However, we must quickly add that He was also rejected by us. Pontius Pilate stands as our "Gentile representative" when he "washed his hands" and would not take responsibility for allowing Jesus Christ to go to the cross. It was not just Israel's sin that crucified Jesus Christ. The responsibility belongs to the whole world! We've all "sinned and fall short of the glory of God" (Rom.3:23). Furthermore, Jesus Christ died for the sins of the whole world (John 3:16).

Fourth, Jesus Christ, like Moses, *prayed for those who nailed Him to the cross.* As we've seen, Moses again and again fell on his face and prayed that God would save the lives of the children of Israel—even when they turned against him. And when Jesus Christ hung on the cross, He looked down on those who had put Him there and said: "Father, forgive them, for they do not know what they are doing" (Luke 23:34).

Becoming God's Man Today

Principles to Live By

What can we learn from both Moses and Jesus Christ regarding handling unjust criticism?

Principle 1. It is not always wrong to defend ourselves against unjust criticism, but we must do it in God's way.

Before the cross, Jesus Christ defended Himself when He was falsely accused—particularly when people questioned who He was (John 5:36–40). The apostle Paul also defended himself against unjust criticism (1 Cor. 9:3–6).

Consequently, it's not wrong to defend ourselves in certain circumstances. However, we must always do so in a non-defensive manner. Our motives should always be primarily to glorify Jesus Christ and His reputation, not ours. Both Jesus Christ and Paul were concerned about God's glory, not theirs. When we defend ourselves, we must always ask ourselves *why*. Is it to protect ourselves, or are we attempting to achieve a higher and more noble goal?

Principle 2. When we defend ourselves, our motives should never be vindictive.

This principle is clearly an extension of the one we've just looked at. When we're falsely accused, we must never allow our anger—which is a very normal, negative emotion—to turn to bitterness. This is why Paul warned the Ephesians: "'In your anger do not sin.' Do not let the sun go down while you are still angry, and do not give the devil a foothold" (Eph. 4:26–27).

Both Moses and Jesus got angry. Though Moses was human and certainly may have sinned in the process, Jesus never did. The point is that anger is normal under certain circumstances. When it happens, however, we should never allow our negative feelings to turn to bitterness or to cause us to try to take vengeance—even on our enemies. Jesus taught that it was better to "turn the other cheek," and Paul warned the Romans never to "repay anyone evil for evil" (Rom 12:17). Expanding on this idea, he wrote: "Do not take revenge, my friends, but leave room for God's wrath, for it is written: 'It is mine to avenge; I will repay,' says the Lord" (12:19).

Principle 3. There are times we should never try to defend ourselves but allow God and others to set the record straight.

Jesus exemplified this principle more than anyone else when He hung on the cross. He knew a time would come when "every knee" would "bow, in heaven and on earth and under the earth." He knew that in a future moment, "every tongue" would "confess that" He is "Lord, to the glory of God the Father" (Phil. 2:10–11). This was not the time! He must wait for his heavenly Father to vindicate him.

There will be times in our own lives when we must wait for our heavenly Father to vindicate us—particularly when we've been falsely accused. When we try to do it ourselves, we'll only make matters worse! We'll play into the hands of our enemies—including Satan!

I remember a time in my own life when I was falsely accused by a group of leaders in the church I pastored. They were men that I had taught and had entrusted with significant responsibility. However, because of their immaturity, their pride, and other sinful patterns of behavior, they falsely accused me—even trying to remove me from the ministry. I tried to defend myself—as did others. However, the situation deteriorated! There came a time I felt I should remove myself completely from the scene and allow God to solve the problem. Even then, there were times when I wanted to expose their sins. However, some very wise men advised me to wait on the Lord and allow Him to defend me. In their wisdom, they knew I would only set myself up for criticism from the larger community since it would be interpreted as vindictiveness.

And so I waited—sometimes impatiently. I would be less than honest if I didn't admit that the Lord and I had some intense conversations—at least on my part. But the time came when God set the record straight. When He did, He exposed immorality, jealousy, and other sinful patterns of behavior. One of the main perpetrators was actually sentenced to prison for attempted rape. Needless to say, when that happened, my own reputation was quickly vindicated—but more importantly, God vindicated His reputation.

I remember the day so clearly when I came face to face with the reality that I couldn't solve this problem on my own. As I searched my heart, I recognized that I wanted to vindicate my name—more than the name of Jesus Christ. I also remember the moment when I told the Lord that His reputation was the most important aspect of this whole crisis. I also acknowledged that He could defend his own name! He did— and when it happened, He defended me too. No one could argue with the results or accuse me of trying to vindicate myself. God set the record straight!

Personalizing These Principles

It's sometimes difficult to know when to defend ourselves against false criticism and when to allow God and others to "speak" for us! Generally speaking, it's always best to have other people verify our character (Prov. 27:2). And when we face a problem that no one can or will correct, we have no choice but to "let go"of the problem and turn it over completely to God, trusting Him to vindicate us. When we come to this point, we can be sure that in His time and in His way, He will set the record straight. In the meantime, Jesus made it clear that we must deal with our own hearts and forgive and pray for our enemies (Matt. 5:43–44; 6:14–15). We must "overcome evil with good" (Rom. 12:21).

Set a Goal

As you reflect on Moses' experience with unjust criticism and on the principles that flow from his life, ask the Holy Spirit to pinpoint one area in your life where you need to set a personal goal:

_____

_____

_____

Memorize the Following Scripture

"You have heard that it was said, 'Love your neighbor and hate your enemy.' But I tell you: Love your enemies and pray for those who persecute you."
MATTHEW 5:43–44

Growing Together

1. Why is it so painful to experience unjust criticism, especially from those we've trusted?

2. Would you share with us how you've handled this kind of criticism—either properly or improperly? If you didn't respond properly, what would you do differently if you could do it all over again?

3. Based on the principles in this study, what additional insights can you give as to when to defend ourselves and when to turn the matter completely over to God?

4. How can we pray for you specifically?

Chapter 13

Never Too Old to Fail

*D*o any of us ever get old enough or wise enough to avoid failure? The answer, of course, is no. For those of us who have been around for a while, this is a scary thought. The possibility of failure becomes even more scary when we see that it happened to Moses, especially in view of his humility and his desire to do the will of God.

However, God deals with reality! That's why He tells us virtually everything about these Old Testament personalities—particularly their failures. In this sense, God keeps no secrets!

It's encouraging, however, to know that we need not fail like Moses and some of the other Old Testament characters. That's why God has recorded these events in such vivid detail. As I've quoted so often in this *Men of Character* series, God made this point clear in His letter to the Corinthians: "These things happened to them *as examples* and were written down *as warnings* for us, on whom the fulfillment of the ages has come. So, if you think you are standing firm, be careful that you don't fall!" (1 Cor. 10:11–12).

Gaining Perspective

When Israel first arrived in Kadesh Barnea, God instructed Moses to send men to spy out the land of Canaan—not to see if Israel could capture the land, but rather to evaluate what they would encounter once they crossed the border (Num. 13:2). Out of the twelve men who went in, all agreed it was a wonderful place—a land flowing with milk and honey. But unfortunately, only two—Joshua and Caleb—felt they could conquer the land.

The other ten men were terribly frightened and reported on the fortified cities and the military strength of the people who lived in Canaan. Their fear was so intense and the report so dismal that it affected all Israel. The people went into a state of rebellion and despair and refused to obey the Lord and to move forward. When Joshua and Caleb tried to convince everyone that they should enter the land, the Israelites became so angry and frustrated they wanted to stone these courageous men—along with Moses and Aaron.

The Lord's patience came to an end! This was the moment they had all been waiting for! And now Israel failed to obey God, to trust Him to give them victory over the Canaanites. God "appeared at the Tent of Meeting" and revealed His glory "to all the Israelites" (14:10). Once again, He was angry with His people and wanted to destroy them all and start over with Moses' family (14:12). But, once again, Moses interceded for Israel. What a faithful shepherd!

Staying true to His promises, God listened to his servant. Rather than striking "them down with a plague," the Lord extended His grace and sentenced Israel to forty years of wandering in the wilderness—a year for every day the spies were in the land. They would have to travel aimlessly until all who were twenty years old and upward died—all those who had witnessed and rejected the Lord's gracious manifestations and miracles (32:11–12). There would be only two exceptions—Joshua and Caleb—because they sincerely wanted to obey the Lord (14:22–30).

Forty Years Later

The years Israel wandered in the wilderness were rather uneventful and probably incredibly boring. We learn very little from the biblical record. In some respects, this is symbolic. Not only was it a wilderness experience environmentally, but it was also a barren and unfruitful existence for Israel spiritually, reflecting "disobedience" and "death." At the same time, a new generation emerged to replace the people who were under God's judgment.

But God did not forsake Israel—even though they forsook Him and continued to worship false gods (Amos 5:25–26; Acts 7:42–43). In spite of their idolatry, God continued to meet their physical needs. At the end of this time of judgment, Moses reminded them: "'During the forty years that I led you through the desert, your clothes did not wear out, nor did the sandals on your feet'" (Deut. 29:5; see also 2:7).

We're not told what went through Moses' mind during these years. We can only speculate. Whatever his thoughts, one thing is certain. He remained faithful to the Lord, and he never forsook Israel as their leader. He accepted God's judgment with his people, even though he was not responsible for their unbelief and disobedience. In fact, he had desperately tried to keep this from happening.

On the other hand, perhaps this barren experience also began to affect Moses spiritually. The mighty miracles he had witnessed so often may have begun to fade in his memory. It's possible he began to slip back into some of his old patterns of thinking and behavior. We must remember that Moses was just a man—and forty years wandering in the wilderness with a group of carnal and sinful people is a long, long time. If these things indeed happened to Moses, it helps explain why he did what he did at the end of the forty-year period.

Moses' Sin

Israel was now back in Kadesh Barnea. They had come full circle. It was the first month of the fortieth year, and they had no water (Num. 20:1–2). Most of them were too young to remember what God had done at Rephidim when Moses struck the rock with his rod and water gushed out (Exod. 17:1–6). And even if they had remembered, this new generation was following closely in the steps of their parents—murmuring, complaining, and forgetting the blessings God was showering upon them daily (Num. 20:3–5).

Both Moses and Aaron—as they had done so many times before—went into the tabernacle to pray for Israel (20:6). Again God had mercy on His people and responded to Moses' prayer with these words: "The LORD said to Moses, 'Take the staff, and you and your brother Aaron gather the assembly together. Speak to that rock before their eyes and it will pour out its water'" (20:7–8).

For the most part, Moses and Aaron obeyed God explicitly. They assembled all of Israel before the rock (20:9). But then Moses departed from God's will. Rather than simply speaking to the rock, he struck it twice (20:11)—angrily crying out to the people: "'Listen, you rebels, must we bring you water out of this rock?'" (20:10).

In his frustration, Moses did several things that displeased the Lord. *First*, he became so angry that he lost control. He reverted to what he did when he first left Pharaoh's court to go out to deliver Israel from bondage. In a fit of rage, he had struck down an Egyptian—an irresponsible act that plagued him for the next forty years.

Second, Moses deliberately disobeyed the Lord. He was to *speak* to the rock. In his anger, he *struck* the rock. The man who had been so cautious and particular about obeying God in every respect, in a moment of weakness, failed to follow the Lord's detailed instructions. The fact that the Lord instructed him to strike the rock at Rephidim forty years earlier was not an acceptable excuse (Exod. 17:6).

Third, Moses exalted himself and his brother Aaron in front of Israel. "'Must *we* bring you water out of this rock?'" he shouted. It is difficult to explain why this great yet humble man responded in this way. At one point, God describes

Moses as "more humble than anyone else on the face of the earth" (Num. 12:3). Perhaps he *had* begun to slip spiritually in his relationship with God during the forty years in the wilderness. Time has a way of dulling our sensitivity to the Lord. Or maybe he felt insecure and a need to demonstrate his position and power with God to this new generation! After all, most of these people had no first-hand experience with the mighty miracles at the Red Sea, at Marah, and at Sinai.

Whatever the reason, at this moment Moses failed God. Unfortunately, the Lord could not overlook the results of this sin—even though He certainly forgave Moses. As Israel's leader, he had set a bad example. If the Lord allowed his actions to go unpunished, it would only encourage this new generation to disobey and doubt God even more than their parents. Consequently, God had to hold Moses accountable. Because of his failure, he would not be able to lead the children of Israel into the land of Canaan (Num. 20:12; 27:12–14). With great responsibility goes great accountability!

Moses' Mature Response

Moses' reaction to God's discipline reflected the man he really was. All of us make mistakes, but only a man of God responds maturely when he's confronted. Predictably, Moses was disappointed. In his humanness, he pleaded with God to change his mind. "'O Sovereign LORD,'" he prayed! "'You have begun to show to your servant your greatness and your strong hand. For what god is there in heaven or on earth who can do the deeds and mighty works you do? Let me go over and see the good land beyond the Jordan'" (Deut. 3:24–25). But this time—and somewhat ironically—the Lord would not change his mind.

No doubt Moses remembered the many times he had prayed for Israel and had influenced the Lord to withdraw his hand of judgment. When God said "no," he may have even been tempted to remind the Lord that Israel's sins were far more serious than his own! But there's no evidence that this temptation got beyond a fleeting thought. Moses accepted God's decision and quickly turned his eyes away from himself and focused his attention once again on God's people. What an act of unselfishness! Again we see the real Moses. He was concerned primarily for Israel's welfare. What would they do without a leader? They would "be like sheep without a shepherd" (Num. 27:17). He immediately asked the Lord to appoint someone to take his place (27:16).

God responded to Moses' prayer and let him know that Joshua would be his successor. Moses was obviously pleased, for here was a young man who had stood by him all the way from Egypt to the border of Canaan. He had served as Moses' "attendant . . . from his youth" (11:28). There's no evidence that Moses ever became jealous or bitter—which often happens when younger men replace older men. The greatest of all Old Testament prophets willingly stepped aside to allow Joshua to lead Israel into the promised land.

Moses' Departure

Even though Moses was not allowed to lead Israel into the land, God partially answered his prayer. He allowed his servant to at least see the land. The Lord Himself conducted Moses on a guided tour to the top of Mount Pisgah. From this vantage point, He showed his faithful servant the land of Canaan (Deut. 34:1–4).

Moses then died. Though he "was a hundred and twenty years old . . . yet his eyes were not weak nor his strength gone" (34:5–7). Moses had begun his career in Israel as a very strong man, and even though he endured unusual stress, he ended his life on earth well-preserved—a great tribute to his trust and confidence in God and an even greater tribute to the Lord's loving care and concern for His friend.

Moses' funeral was extraordinary. Most people are buried by other men. Moses was interred by the God of the universe (34:6). Actually, some people believe he may have been transported bodily to heaven like Elijah—who was taken to heaven in the midst of a whirlwind (2 Kings 2:11).

Whatever the circumstances, Moses' death and burial was glorious. He went to spend eternity with his Heavenly Father where he would never commit another sin or make another mistake. There he would be eternally rewarded for his faithfulness as a leader in Israel. There, too, he would never face another moment of anger, sorrow, unjust criticism, or disappointment. He would also have the wonderful privilege of appearing on another mountain in the presence of God—the Mount of Transfiguration. It happened after God came to earth in the form of a man and revealed the glory of God (John 1:14). There he, along with another Old Testament great named Elijah, appeared with Jesus Christ. Three New Testament apostles—Peter, James, and John—looked on and heard the voice of God coming from another cloud and saying, "'This is my Son, whom I love; with Him I am well pleased. Listen to Him!'" (Matt. 17:1–6). Think of the thrill this must have been for Moses! He now fully understood why he had to suffer—it was for Jesus Christ! He had received "his reward" (Heb. 11:26).

The children of Israel mourned and wept for Moses for thirty days (Deut. 34:8). When all was said and done, they realized that they had lost a great leader. Sadly, they had to wait until he died to realize what a great man Moses really was! In many respects, he could not be replaced—which is verified by the Lord's final tribute to this man of God. It serves as one of the most significant epithets in history. Furthermore, it is not recorded on a lonely tombstone in a secluded mountain cave but in the eternal Word of God: "Since then, no prophet has risen in Israel like Moses, whom the LORD knew face to face, who did all those miraculous signs and wonders the LORD sent him to do in Egypt—to

Pharaoh and to all his officials and to his whole land. For no one has ever shown the mighty power or performed the awesome deeds Moses did in the sight of all Israel" (34:10–12).

Becoming God's Man Today

Principles to Live By

There are two very important principles we can learn and apply from this final installment in Moses' life story. The first is definitely a warning—a lesson we all need to learn. The second principle is a very comforting reality.

Principle 1. We are never too old or too wise to fail God.

No matter how close we are to God and how many answers we have had to prayer, no matter how much God has used us, we can still, in a moment of weakness, sin against God. In other words, no matter how faithful we have been, we have no guarantee that we will not blow it in the homestretch. This is why the apostle warned the Corinthians—and us all: "So, if you think you're standing firm, be careful that you don't fall!" (1 Cor. 10:12).

Principle 2. We have all the resources we need to keep us from failing God—now and in the homestretch of life.

Perhaps you're thinking, if Moses failed, how can it *not* happen to me? Be encouraged! This is why God has recorded these events—including both Israel's sins as well as Moses' disobedience. This is the whole thrust of what Paul was writing to the Corinthians, which bears repeating: "These things happened to them as examples and were written down as warnings for us" (10:11).

Paul then follows this exhortation with a wonderful promise: "*No temptation has seized you except what is common to man. And God is faithful; he will not let you be tempted beyond*

*what you can bear. But when you are tempted, he will also provide
a way out so that you can stand up under it" (10:13).*

As Christians, we are not destined to fail. God has provided a way out. We can "be strong in the Lord and in His
mighty power" by putting "on the full armor of God" so
that we "can take" our "stand against the devil's schemes"
(Eph. 6:10–18).

Personalizing These Principles

This final section is designed to be a brief review of Moses' life
and the major lessons that flow from his experience with God
and the children of Israel. It will give you an opportunity to
reconfirm your desire to be a more mature Christian man—a
man of character. As you read over the following statements,
check those that have impacted your life the most:

❏ Like Moses' father, I want to be wise and discern-
   ing—a man who has faith in God, and courage to
   always do what is right, as well as a parent who has
   developed a careful strategy to rear my children in
   God's ways (Exod. 2:1–10).

❏ Like Moses, I want to make the right choices in life—
   choices to serve God and to put Jesus Christ at the center of my life, no matter what the cost (Heb. 11:24–26).

❏ I want to learn from Moses' mistakes—to be motivated more by reason than by emotion; to avoid trying
   to do God's work in my own strength; to avoid having
   to suffer rejection because of my own foolish mistakes
   (Exod. 2:11–15; Acts 7:23–29).

❏ I often identify with Moses' inferiority complex on the
   backside of the desert. But by God's grace, I want to
   respond to God, realizing that He can use me in spite of
   my human weaknesses (Exod. 2:23–25; 3:1–22; 4:1–20).

❏ As Moses allowed God to rebuild his self-image, I also want to allow God to rebuild mine—no matter how painful the process (Exod. 4:27–14:31).

❏ Like Moses, I always want to honor and glorify God for all my successes and achievements in life (Exod. 15:1–18).

❏ Like Moses, I want to learn to become a good manager of my own household as well as all other areas of responsibility (Exod. 18:1–27).

❏ When everyone else around me is inconsistent and fickle, I want to be a faithful and consistent Christian— just like Moses was when all Israel turned to idolatry (Exod. 32:1–35).

❏ Like Moses, I want to get to know God better, realizing that I can enter into his very presence as a friend with a friend (Exod. 33:1–23).

❏ Like Moses, I want my life to reflect the glory and goodness of God because I spend time in his pres- ence—listening to His voice from the Scriptures and obeying what He says (Exod. 34:27–35).

❏ Like Moses, I want to handle depression and disap- pointment as a mature Christian, not feeling guilty for things I shouldn't—but quickly confessing my sins when I'm at fault, and then accepting God's perfect for- giveness (Num. 11: 1–25).

❏ Like Moses, I want to learn to handle criticism—par- ticularly unjust criticism—with a mature attitude, defending myself when appropriate, but ultimately allowing God to vindicate me and discipline those who are at fault (Num. 12:1–16; 16:1–35).

❏ I want to constantly be on guard against failure in my Christian life, realizing that God has provided a way to escape temptation's power (Num. 20:1–13; Deut. 34:1–12; 1 Cor. 10:11–13).

Set a Goal

What one personal need has the Holy Spirit impressed on your heart—particularly in this final chapter of Moses' life? Based on this need, set a goal.

_____

_____

_____

Memorize the Following Scripture

No temptation has seized you except what is common to man. And God is faithful; he will not let you be tempted beyond what you can bear. But when you are tempted, He will also provide a way out so that you can stand up under it.

1 CORINTHIANS 10:13

Growing Together

1. Why is it important, particularly as we grow older, to keep our guard up against what John describes as the influence of the world—"the cravings of sinful man, the lust of his eyes and the boasting of what he has and does" (1 John 2:16)?

2. What are some of the worldly "land mines" Satan has crafted for men particularly? How can we avoid these "land mines"?

3. What have you learned about temptation as you've grown older?

4. Would you be willing to share how Satan has at times trapped you?

5. How can we pray for you specifically?

Endnotes

Chapter 2

1. Mike Bauman, *Greatest Sports Dynasties* (The Sporting News Publishing Company, 1989), 94.

Chapter 7

1. For an in-depth study of these characteristics outlined by Paul in 1 Timothy 3 and Titus 1 see Gene A. Getz, *The Measure of a Man* (Ventura, Calif.: Regal Books).

Chapter 11

1. For another biblical perspective on how to handle depression, see Gene A. Getz, *Elijah: Remaining Steadfast Through Uncertainty* (Nashville: Broadman & Holman Publishers)